Exploring Haydn

WITHDRAWN

Unlocking the Masters Series, No. 6

Exploring Haydn

A Listener's Guide to Music's Boldest Innovator

David Hurwitz

AMADEUS
PRESS

Enclosed compact discs:
CDs 1 and 2 (excluding CD 2, track 16): Musical recordings under license from Naxos of America, www.naxos.com. All rights reserved. Unlawful duplication, broadcast or performance of these discs is prohibited by applicable law.
CD 2, track 16: Recording licensed under permission of Hänssler Classic, Max-Eyth-Str.41, D-71088 Holzgerlingen, Germany. All rights reserved.

Published in 2005 by

Amadeus Press, LLC
512 Newark Pompton Turnpike
Pompton Plains, New Jersey 07444, USA

For sales, please contact

NORTH AMERICA

AMADEUS PRESS, LLC
c/o Hal Leonard Corp.
7777 West Bluemound Road
Milwaukee, Wisconsin 53213, USA
Phone: 800-637-2852
Fax: 414-774-3259

E-mail: orders@amadeuspress.com
Website: www.amadeuspress.com

UNITED KINGDOM AND EUROPE

ROUNDHOUSE PUBLISHING LTD.
Millstone, Limers Lane
Northam, North Devon EX39 2RG, UK
Phone: 01237-474474
E-mail: roundhouse.group@ukgateway.net

Printed in Canada

Library of Congress Cataloging-in-Publication Data

Hurwitz, David.
  Exploring Haydn : a listener's guide to music's boldest innovator / David Hurwitz.
    p. cm. -- (Unlocking the masters series ; No. 6)
  ISBN 1-57467-116-2
  1. Haydn, Joseph, 1732-1809--Criticism and interpretation. I. Title. II. Series.

  MT92.H2H87 2005
  780'.92--dc22
                                    2005024904

To Sören Meyer-Eller: a true friend

My calling has no limits; what may yet be done in music is far greater than what has already been done. . . .
—Joseph Haydn on the occasion
of his seventy-fourth birthday

No one does it all—jokes and surprises, laughter and profound emotion—and all this as well as Haydn.
—W. A. Mozart

Ach! If I had only become a critic, how much I would have found to criticize!
—Joseph Haydn

Contents

Part 3
A Topical View

Preface

*Think of me as a man to whom God has given talent and a
good heart. I make no greater claims.*

—Joseph Haydn

Haydn isn't just the least listened to of the three great composers (with Mozart and Beethoven) who comprise the so-called
First Viennese School. He's also the least read about, which
is a pity, because of the three, he is in many respects the best
documented. With a lengthy history of employment by a major
aristocratic family that kept meticulous records, a voluminous
international correspondence, and a long life recorded in no less
than three contemporary biographies, there's plenty for scholars
to pick over and for interested music lovers to enjoy. As the most
famous living composer in his day, he was, moreover, "news."
Contemporary sources have an inimitable flavor and immediacy,
placing the reader in closer contact with the man and his era than
anything else can.

So in addition to quoting Haydn's own letters, gracefully
translated by H. C. Robbins Landon in his monumental study
Haydn: Chronicle and Works (Indiana University Press, 1978), I
begin most chapters with a few relevant lines taken from Georg
August Griesinger's *Biographische Notizen über Joseph Haydn,* first
published in 1809, the year of the composer's death. Griesinger
was the most succinct, as well as arguably the most accurate, of
Haydn's contemporary biographers. He enjoyed a close friendship
with the old man and seems to have had no agenda other than to
report what he actually heard Haydn say. This doesn't mean that

the composer, with his memory slowly failing, always got the facts right himself, but that isn't really anything that readers of a nonacademic survey such as this need worry about.

I have translated Griesinger's (and Haydn's) comments freely from the original German, and I hope that they convey additional insight into a man who, however modest and unassuming, was an exceptionally astute and self-aware artist. Haydn's remarks about himself and music in general deserve to be taken very seriously by anyone seeking to get better acquainted with his work, and they shed a remarkable light on the motivations and surprisingly contemporary aesthetic of an artist too often taken for granted and treated with condescension. Besides, they're very enjoyable to read in and of themselves. It seems that Haydn just couldn't help being entertaining.

Introduction

There is no composer in the history of music who achieved the astonishing progression that we may observe in Haydn's music from the Missa brevis *in F of c. 1749 to the* Harmonienmesse *of 1802. There have been, of course, many composers who went through a similar development in their artistic careers—Monteverdi, Domenico Scarlatti, Gluck and Beethoven are names that spring to mind. But the road that Haydn had to travel is longer than that taken by any of his predecessors, contemporaries, or successors. From Symphony No. 1 to Symphony No.104, or from the* Salve Regina *in E (1756) to the* Te Deum *for the Empress Marie Therese (1799–1800), Haydn's style underwent a metamorphosis almost unparalleled in any of the arts, let alone music. It is actually difficult to realize that the same man composed the late Baroque music of the* Missa brevis *in F and the prelude to "Winter" from* The Seasons *(1801). And not only was it composed by the same man, but that creator, starting as an almost anonymous figure in the galaxy of Viennese music c. 1750, invented the string quartet as we know it today, became the Father of the Symphony—the Germans called him that in 1800, even knowing that there were many predecessors in the symphonic field before Haydn—and the founder of what may be called the greatest school in the history of music.*

So writes the great Haydn scholar H. C. Robbins Landon, and his words are so succinctly apt that it's impossible not to quote them right from the start. They also suggest the reason that any book on Haydn necessarily requires a series of compromises and choices that, one way or another, make it very difficult to do justice to the creative genius of such an important and musically fascinating figure. The problem is simple: most composers have distinctive mature styles that can be neatly categorized (or nearly so). Such is the case, for example, with Mozart, much of whose early music (and we're talking about hundreds of pieces) can be conveniently ignored without losing anything of value on which his reputation rests.

Haydn, however, represents the artistic equivalent of a moving target. He was the Thomas Edison of music. Like Edison, Haydn combined endless curiosity with an inexhaustible imagination and a phenomenal capacity for sheer hard work. Like Edison, his life was one of ceaseless experimentation and invention, of problems surmounted and challenges met. No prodigy as a composer in the Mozartian sense nor a quick or facile worker, Haydn was twenty-seven when he wrote his First Symphony, and from the 1750s onwards, he produced masterpieces in any one of several fully characteristic and mature musical styles. So even though, for instance, most concertgoers will be familiar with a few of his late symphonies, the fact is that *early* does not mean "immature" or "inferior," as it does with so many other composers.

Furthermore, for those who love his music, aside from the inherent pleasure of considering favorite works individually, part of the unique joy to be found in Haydn—and practically nowhere else—rests in the opportunity to follow his evolution as an artist from the great early works to the great late ones, secure in the knowledge that the quality will remain consistent along the entire journey. This makes leaving anything out a sad necessity for the writer, even though just covering the basics of Haydn's massive output, as I propose to do here, presents all but the most fanatical listeners with an imposing deluge of music clamoring for their time and attention. I know this because it was Haydn who got me hooked on classical music in the first place.

The piece was Symphony No. 88. I was about seven and already enthusiastically exploring my parents' record collection. Aside from the catchy tunes and their attention-grabbing presentation, what particularly captivated me was the *trio* (middle section) of the third-movement minuet (CD 1, track 3 at 1:58). The bagpipe imitations from the low strings and bassoons, the lazily chirping oboe tune, the irregular phrasing and surprising use of rhythm and accent—this was all new to me. Haydn was quite literally painting in tones, creating a magical pastoral scene, and the point was that not only did I love the pure sound of it (I've always enjoyed bagpipes), I instinctively *understood* what it meant. That music without words could communicate feelings and even images so vividly was a revelation to me, and from that moment on, I was determined to hear more, not just of Haydn, but of anything else of a similar nature that I could.

I was lucky in this first encounter, because no composer offers a better place to start one's exploration of classical music than does Haydn. This is precisely because his genius was so comprehensive, his style so open and eclectic, that there is very little in earlier music that he did not absorb and transform and of later music that he did not either invent outright or anticipate. Of all of the great composers, Haydn is the funniest, the most boisterous and energetic, and the most surprising. He is also the most considerate of his listeners, writing in a user-friendly style that never panders, preaches, or lowers its standards one iota in order to make its expressive points.

Stylistically speaking, at all periods Haydn thrives on extremes: of dynamics, for example, and of course tempo, but also in terms of formal variety and actual content. He was both the greatest master of musical counterpoint after Bach (according to Robbins Landon) and the man who demonstrated that folk tunes and ethnic music deserved an honored place in "high art." He is the only major composer to have custom written a national anthem that is still in use today: the "Emperor's Hymn," currently the national anthem of Germany. Russian composer Rimsky-Korsakov considered Haydn to be the most accomplished symphonic orchestrator who ever lived, and as the creator of such colorful works as *Sheherazade* and the *Capriccio espagnol,* he should know. These various popular and sophisticated elements mingle freely in practically each and every work to a degree that would not be seen in music again until nearly a century after Haydn's death, when Mahler once again redefined the parameters of what sort of materials classical music could absorb.

In general, I dislike biographical essays. More often than not they have little to do with giving modern listeners the proper tools to enjoy music whose most important quality is not its relationship (often highly speculative) to events in the composer's life but rather its continued newness and relevance today. However, because Haydn is such an important and comparatively little-known figure, I offer a special chapter (the third) called "Haydn in His Own Words." This lets Haydn introduce himself to you in a selection of letters and quotations that offer a good sense of his character and personality. I have placed this chapter after the first detailed descriptions of Haydn's compositional style so that it is the music that throws light on the man rather than the more usual other way around. Reading about him with his special sound in your ears can only deepen your understanding and appreciation of his achievement.

Haydn's reputation rests primarily on his series of instrumental works, particularly on the symphonies, string quartets, piano sonatas, and piano trios. In the field of vocal music, he's best known for his sacred works and the two magnificent late oratorios. These pieces, therefore, constitute the basis of the discussion in parts 1, 2 and 3, but because there's so much music to cover and Haydn's stylistic evolution was so dramatic, I have decided to take a different approach from the usual survey of instrumental and vocal genres individually, in sequence.

Instead, after pointing out the most important characteristics of his personal style in part 1, in the process canvassing his innovative discoveries in the field of musical form, I will take you in part 2 through two CDs' worth of movements from works written throughout Haydn's creative life. In this way, you can hear how the various expressive styles and ideas that he invented apply to music in all the various genres in which he worked. In part 3, you will find more general discussions that approach the music topically, exploring such issues as Haydn's substantial and still underrated achievement as a composer of vocal music, a survey of some solitary masterpieces that fall outside the main categories of instrumental works, and a discussion of how he was able to capture and portray both tragic and comic emotions as his personal idiom evolved.

Finally, at the end of this book, you will find four appendices listing all the symphonies, quartets, piano sonatas, and piano trios according to their common numberings, keys, and dates of composition. I also include, alongside this basic information, tables of distinguishing characteristics shared by the various works that should prove useful in planning your own collecting and listening strategies, and these tables also serve to summarize the main themes and ideas discussed in the course of this book. Rather than clogging up the text with multiple variants of "See appendix X for the works featuring characteristic Y," I ask you to simply keep this in mind as you read. If you want to hear works where Haydn uses folk music or places the minuet movement second, or if you are interested in the output of a particular period, just refer to the appendices for a quick list. The total result of all this (I hope) will be an approach in which as many works and ways of enjoying them are discussed as possible, within a convenient format.

Part 1

Extraordinary Musician, Ordinary Man

Inventing Music
as We Know It
(and Why This Turned Out
to Be a Mixed Blessing)

I sit down at the keyboard and begin to improvise, happy or sad, as my mood dictates, serious or frivolous. When I grasp an idea, my entire effort then is devoted towards developing and elaborating it according to the principles of art. Early on I resolved to continue working in this manner, and it is here that so many new composers come up short. They line up one little bit after the other, and stop before they have scarcely started, so that after listening nothing stays in one's heart.

—Joseph Haydn

Listeners coming to Haydn having lived long with Mozart (or some of the more famous composers of the romantic period) may find themselves disappointed initially, because despite many points in common, the two differ in one crucial respect: their handling of tunes. Mozart was, first and foremost, a tune-smith, a specialist in the writing of singable melodies, while Haydn was a generalist and an eclectic—at least in the instrumental works for which he is most highly valued today (the vocal pieces are another matter entirely). His specialty, if he can be said to have had one, was probably harmony: arresting, affecting, and always surprising. There's no getting around this fact, and it needs to be addressed up front. But what does it mean in practical terms? Certainly not that Haydn's themes aren't memorable, beautiful, or expressive—they are all that, and more.

The idea that the same man who composed the national anthem of both Austria (originally) and Germany (currently) might have had a problem writing tunes with mass appeal is patently ridiculous. Haydn was also, first and foremost, a very well-trained singer. This issue, then, has less to do with Haydn's ability to create melodies in vocal style than it does with describing the many kinds of themes and materials one finds in his instrumental works. In fact, Haydn has a huge variety of melodic types as well as an extremely wide expressive range—arguably wider than Mozart's, whose treatment of his tunes can be less important than their immediate emotional effect. These are gross generalizations, granted, but useful nonetheless for the light they shed on two composers so alike in some ways but also fundamentally different in others.

Over the course of a movement or work, Haydn's tunes frequently change their emotional stripes. He delights in showing how they can evoke many different, even opposite, feelings from one moment to the next as they appear in varying harmonic perspectives. This accounts for his broad range of reference and variety of expression (not to mention a good bit of his sense of humor). And there's nothing particularly obscure or unusual about Haydn's technique. In fact, it helps ensure that his music remains interesting over its entire span. The notion that a composer has recourse to a special style when writing for instruments instead of voices, and so asks for a slightly different perspective when listening, doesn't mean that the works in question are any less approachable or immediately appealing. The key to understanding lies in knowing what to expect. That is the goal of this chapter: to suggest where best to focus your attention. In order to do this, I am going to unflinchingly confront the dreaded "f" word: that is to say, *form*—and specifically, *sonata form*.

The word *sonata,* which simply comes from the Italian, meaning "sound," has several meanings. At various times, you might hear it used in reference to a genre, a style, or a specific formal type. In Haydn's day, the genre definition of sonata meant basically "any piece of instrumental music having a movement in sonata form," and it didn't matter if this was a symphony, concerto, string quartet, piano trio, solo, duo, or anything else. All are sonatas, whether or not the word actually appears in their title. When it comes to the stylistic and formal parameters of the classical sonata, matters become a bit more complicated, largely owing to the disparity between the convenient textbook definition of sonata form and what the composers using it actually did.

It's always risky when it comes to questions of musical form to claim that anyone "invented" anything, if this means "discovered or used it for the first time ever." Even so, if Haydn cannot be said to have invented sonata form, he certainly perfected it, and he was the first composer to understand its potential and exploit it to the fullest possible extent. Most experts on the subject would probably agree that without his example, the music of his best friend, Mozart; his pupil Beethoven; and all the great composers who followed him would scarcely have taken the shape that it did. In particular, the symphony and the string quartet likely would never have come to occupy their current positions of eminence in the orchestral and chamber genres, respectively. So in this sense at least, Haydn really did invent music as we know it today.

Unfortunately, few concepts in Western music have been so poorly presented to the music-loving public as sonata form, especially in considering the works of Haydn. Ironically, he became a victim of his own success. Because the forms and media he either invented or perfected became the foundation of so much music by later composers, sometimes in radically different styles, listeners armed with this information expect Haydn to actually sound like those others, when in fact he sounds most like himself. His individuality has been obscured by his unique historical position as the founder of Western civilization's greatest and most important musical "school."

So the first important point to understand is that the *sonata principle,* Haydn's biggest formal discovery, is not so much a concrete set of rules or a specific "form" as it is a general concept that permitted unprecedented freedom of expression and, above all, the personalization of music according to each composer's individual style and taste. For this reason, it was, and remains, an absolutely stupendous invention, a genuine landmark in the history of the arts and a truly beautiful thing, happily not at all difficult to grasp. The most noteworthy qualities of the sonata principle—its elegance, flexibility, and practicality—all arise from just a few common-sense ideas.

1. The Idea of Departure and Return

The ability to perceive musical form rests on the way in which composers arrange their material: on repetition (to aid memory), variation (to explore the expressive possibilities of the material), and contrast (to avoid stiffness and monotony). When you listen to any traditional (i.e., not avant-garde) tonal piece of music, whether a simple song or a long symphony, you will notice that certain tunes or motives appear in alternation with different material, but most movements or works end with a return either to the opening themes or to some element of the music that you have heard before. This automatically creates the impression of arrival at a goal and satisfaction at the ending eventually achieved. Indeed, this fact is so obvious that it seems hardly worth mentioning.

In this respect, the sonata principle is no different from music in many other forms, large or small. What makes it unique, though, is the impression that it creates of physical, forward movement through time and the emphasis it gives to the "departure and return" concept. Sonata forms (for there are many different varieties) give composers a blueprint that allows them to use as many themes or ideas as they like, explore them at length, make their reappearance correspondingly exciting and effective, and present the whole shebang as a progressive, evolving sequence of interrelated events. The sonata principle does all this without ever losing the logical thread that binds an entire movement together as a single, harmonious whole, while at the same time making it easy for listeners to follow the musical journey from the beginning to its emotionally satisfying end.

2. The Idea of Location

Any formal principle based on the notion of departure and return accepts as given the fact that there must be a point of origin as well as a measure of distance traveled. Without these, it would be impossible to hear any sort of ongoing musical progress whatsoever. Music, though, is not geography but a succession of sounds in time. However, it does have a unique equivalent to the geographical concept of place: *tonality,* or *key.* This extremely intimidating and vexatious subject, often raised in connection with the abstruse terminology of harmonic analysis, owes most of its fear factor to the work of writers and music theorists who tend to describe music solely in harmonic terms to the exclusion of all else. Such discussions say practically nothing about what the music actually sounds like from the perspective of a listener hearing it as it plays.

Apart from distinguishing the emotional qualities of the *major* (happy) and *minor* (sad) modes, most people without perfect pitch aren't even conscious of individual keys—there are twenty-four in our tonal system, half major, half minor—unless a composer make a special expressive point of the contrast between them. Whenever one writes a tune or motive, this also defines a key, and if this is the main theme of the movement, then listeners will naturally associate both the key and the theme that occupies it with the work's musical starting point, or "home." Staying in the same key for a long period of time, however, quickly becomes dull and sounds uneventful, while on the other hand, repeating the same tune in a new key makes the melody sound fresh and different, and so justifies the repetition. Changing key (or *modulating*), therefore, is an important means of contrast, and essential in any longer music in order to sustain the listener's interest. Often a change of key accompanies the introduction of completely new material as well. Progress from one key to the next imparts the sensation of movement away from the starting point—that is, of departure.

3. The Idea of Delay, Surprise, Suspense, and Fulfillment

Once the composer has presented a series of themes and established the impression of motion away from the initial, home key (called the *tonic*), he often doesn't want to return immediately and bring the music to a rapid conclusion. What can he do to delay this event creatively, providing maximum musical interest and expressive power? The answer is: just about anything. All the means of providing musical contrast come into play: surprising changes in volume, texture, speed, phrasing, and rapid movement through many keys; introduction of new material, variations of old material, sudden interruptions, suspenseful pauses, moments of high tension, climaxes, and alternating periods of relaxation. There are no rules as to what composers can do. Their choice of options depends on how well they understand the potential of the thematic material with which they choose to work, but there are some very important considerations that give a pretty good indication of what a competent musician is likely to try.

Most of the tactics mentioned have in common the fact that they belong to the general category of "interruption." Delaying the return to the home key and its familiar themes is in fact quite easy in theory. The problem (and the art) rests not with the delay as much as in maintaining continuity despite all the disruptive activity going on at any given time. One way to address this issue is to limit the actual thematic material during this "delayed return" episode to themes and motives heard so far. This has the dual advantage of establishing an audible connection to what has come before and also presenting the older material in a way that explores its expressive potential. New themes can always be introduced to provide additional contrast if needed. Any remaining questions of continuity can be resolved by adhering more or less closely to the rules of modulation in moving from one key to the next. These are quite technical, but all you need to know is that transitions can either be smooth or abrupt and that good composers know which kind they want, as well as how and when to use them.

Once the composer feels he has spent a sufficient amount of time delaying the moment of return and the actual event finally arrives, one last challenge remains: that of creating a conclusion satisfying in its feeling of finality after so long a period of instability. Again the solution is very sensible. Rather than moving away from home, as the thematic material did originally, simply rewrite it so that even the sections that modulated to different keys remain in the initial, tonic key—however much they may give evidence of wanting to go elsewhere.

Continued harping on the stability of the main key will confirm, if only subconsciously, that the movement must be drawing to a close, even when the original tunes have changed considerably from their initial appearance. This fundamental musical fact is completely unavoidable, because it engages your memory, not just of the themes themselves, but also of the keys that they initially defined. It's a quality inherent in our system of tonal music, and this is the reason you don't need to have any special knowledge of keys or harmony in order to experience its audible effects and understand its expressive point.

The Textbook Definition

Because the sonata principle utilizes as its basis the idea of departure and return, movements written in so-called *sonata form* are often (logically) called *binary*—that is, they have two parts, one departing and the other returning. Both these halves may be repeated, which makes the form particularly clear but also obviously increases the length of the movement. On the other hand, since the second part has two purposes, an episode of delay followed by the fulfillment of the final return to the initial key, the textbook definition of sonata form describes these movements as having three sections overall: *exposition* (departure), *development* (delay), and *recapitulation* (return/fulfillment). The exposition, in turn, consists of a first subject group in the home (tonic) key, followed by a passage of transition leading to a second subject group in a closely related subsidiary key (usually a fifth above the tonic, in which case it is called the *dominant*).

This formal duality has an interesting consequence: including both repeats (where indicated) in performance emphasizes a movement's two-part structure, while omitting the so-called second-half repeat, the general practice today, stresses the division into three sections. In many of his late works, Haydn himself finally dropped the second-half repeat in sonata-form movements, but he then often substitutes a sort of "second-half repeat

equivalent" in the form of a first-movement coda—sometimes
brief, sometimes lengthy and consisting of entirely fresh developments, but invariably leading to an even more emphatic reestab-
lishment of the tonic key. This sacrifices none of the advantages of
the repeat in reinforcing the feeling of return, while providing an
opportunity for new expressive revelations, as well as an equally
satisfying final climax.

A major innovation at the time and one that Beethoven seized
on with particular relish, Haydn's practice set the pattern for
virtually all future instrumental and symphonic music. It partly
accounts for the textbook definition's emphasis on a tripartite
understanding of sonata form, and also for the fact that these large
sectional repeats have primarily been viewed by later generations
as optional and a matter of personal taste, even in earlier music—
a pity in Haydn (not so much in Mozart) because his movements
are almost always written in the expectation that the repeats will
be followed. In other words, they serve a genuine structural function related to the concepts of surprise, delay, and fulfillment.
With the rise of the "period performance practice" movement,
full repeats have been making a comeback as of late, and you
may well encounter them once again, particularly on recordings.

Either way, these technical terms—exposition, development, and recapitulation—are very unsatisfactory. "Exposition"
suggests that the initial presentation of themes contains all the
material for the remainder of the movement, which as often as
not isn't true. "Development" implies some kind of purely intellectual or mechanical process in what is often the movement's
most emotionally intense, adventurous, and capricious part.
"Recapitulation" emphasizes the sameness of the repetition of
what has come before, when one of the most important aspects
of the sonata principle resides in the fact that the initial material
will *not* be repeated literally but changed, often extensively, so
as to emphasize the feeling of returning home.

Far better than the textbook terminology just described, it's both easier and more accurate to think of movements using the sonata principle as consisting of two kinds of music: tunes and motives that define a key and live within it, and "motion music" that travels (or modulates) from one key to the next. Many sonata movements actually use more of the latter than the former, and the transitional ideas are often every bit as active in the development sections. If this sounds confusing, don't worry: it will become immediately clear when actually listening, and because the terms *exposition, development,* and *recapitulation* have become the accepted vocabulary of sonata form, I will use them for the sake of convenience—but please keep in mind the caveats noted.

The sonata principle actually dramatizes purely instrumental music, permitting composers to write pieces according to an inner narrative of feelings and emotions. Themes set out on a journey, undergo a series of adventures, and return, often recognizably, yet changed by their experiences in various ways. They acquire definite emotional qualities, even personalities of sorts, and it is an artist's ability to customize his chosen material that primarily defines his individual musical style: that special sound belonging to no one else. Haydn is especially strong in this kind of originality, because as one of the very few composers of the epoch whose works were not written to show off his own strengths as a performing virtuoso, he had to create music that would express its individual character as interpreted by others. In the sonata style, he found the best way to achieve this goal.

There is yet another remarkable fact absolutely unique to pieces adopting the sonata principle: you almost always know where you are in them. The music's linear, sequential structure necessarily reveals as it unfolds whether any given section belongs to the beginning, the middle, or the end. Knowing where you are in a movement engages your attention at an entirely different level than that of merely recognizing themes as they are repeated and varied when the music is played. It establishes an ongoing relationship between the listener and the unfolding musical form, making the experience more involving, because the composer can create a huge amount of dramatic tension and surprise by gratifying or frustrating expectations as to where the tonal drama is heading. This type of music draws the listener in just as a good story does, by relating not merely what happens but also how it happens, through the author's control over the pace and order of the events being described—in other words, through twists in the plot. In this way, a work's form becomes just as riveting and expressive as its melodic content, and pieces composed utilizing the sonata principle are the only ones about which this observation is generally true.

From Theory to Reality

Example 1
Symphony No. 90 in C Major (1788)

First Movement: Adagio—Allegro assai (CD 1, Track 5)
Scoring: 1 flute, 2 oboes, 2 bassoons, 2 horns in high C,
*   2 trumpets, timpani, and strings*

I chose this movement, full of brilliant color and animal high spirits, because it comes from one of the least known of Haydn's late symphonies. The work has no nickname, and you will probably never encounter it in concert. Nevertheless, the symphony is a masterpiece and so characteristic of Haydn that once you have heard it, you will surely wonder why music so exciting and original remains largely the secret pleasure of a privileged few. Here is a bare-bones outline of its form:

Introduction

Exposition   First Subject (at 0:55)
                                Motion Music (at 1:14)
                                Second Subject (at 1:38)
                                Motion Music (at 1:56)
                                (Exposition repeated)

Development   First Subject (at 4:15)
                                Motion Music (at 4:23)
                                Second Subject (at 4:32)
                                First Subject (at 4:56)
                                Motion Music (at 5:06)

Recapitulation   First Subject (at 5:22)
                                Second Subject (at 5:51)
                                Motion Music (at 6:14)
                                Coda (at 6:41)

I set out the movement's structure in this fashion, first so you can listen straight through a couple of times and experience the music fresh (it's only about six and a half minutes long) and second so you can see just how primitive and uninteresting sonata form looks when reduced to a simple succession of sectional divisions and subdivisions. It's the content that matters. What would you say, for instance, if I told you that the above structure permits Haydn to create a movement consisting of, among other things, a very amusing extended joke at the expense of the first subject?

The first witticisms appear right at the start. Here is a completely accurate verbal representation of the opening adagio:

"Ta-dahhh!... plonk, plonk... plonk, plonk... Plonk! Plonk!"

Yes, it's silly, but the first thing to keep in mind when listening to Haydn is that when something sounds strange or silly, that's because it really *is* strange or silly, and if it makes you smile or laugh, then you are definitely "getting it."

After this goofy opening, a quiet cadence motive (at 0:16)

establishes an atmosphere of calm. A *cadence* is simply a musical term for a closing formula or ending. It marks the conclusion of a musical sentence or paragraph, usually by making a decisive return to the home key of the section in question, and this one has six repeated notes followed by a short descending phrase. Pay special attention to this motive, and note that although it sounds very much like an ending, the music doesn't end. In fact, it continues lazily with a series of sighing descending two- and three-note phrases. The music gently runs out of steam, and the allegro kicks in (at 0:55) with . . .

Exposition

First Subject

. . . the cadence again, only speeded up to the new tempo. The first subject, then, is based on the music of the introduction, and not just in that shared cadence motive, which once again fails to provide an ending. The music blithely continues with two seven-note "squiggles" on the oboes followed by a seven-note shout for the full orchestra, also developing a feature from the introduction. Remember the "plonks"—two quiet two-note phrases then a loud one, all in the same rhythm? This idea isn't a tune but a dynamic pattern: soft–soft–loud. Haydn makes the relationship even clearer by following this modified, busier version of that pattern with the cadence motive once again, exactly as happened in the introduction. These first few seconds of quick music reveal a tremendous amount of information about Haydn's compositional method.

The most important things to remember are that an "idea" in music need not necessarily be a long, regular melody, and that in sonata movements there are no rules as to what constitutes a "subject." It may contain any number of tunes, motives, and gestures, in any combination. This first subject does have a clear shape: ABA, but A is the cadence motive and B is the squiggle—squiggle—shout sequence of gestures. The effect of the music is almost visual, and these tiny motives, so different and so distinctly profiled, appear as individual characters, as indeed they behave throughout the remainder of the movement.

The next important point to understand is that despite the fact that we are technically in the exposition section, the music has actually been developing from the very first bar, a fact that you will find quite typical of Haydn. The cadence motive has already appeared in two versions (slow, then fast), as has the soft—soft—loud sequence (phrases of two notes, then seven). Only notice: the main ideas of the first subject originate in the introduction, technically *before* the beginning of the exposition. Finally, pay particular attention to the fact that the cadence motive begins with a group of repeated notes (six in this case). One of Haydn's most distinctive melodic or motivic fingerprints, this becomes a source of both dramatic surprise and structural continuity.

In all of Haydn's sonata movements, ideas are designed not just to catch the ear on first hearing but also to serve the music's larger expressive purpose. Nothing could be simpler, for example, than beginning a motive or melody with a small bunch of repeated notes. Haydn wants you to follow him and enjoy the music's unfolding story, and whether you are conscious of the details or not, that is exactly what happens as you listen.

Motion Music (at 1:14)

Once again the orchestra ignores the cadence theme's suggestion that the beginning really is the end, and an explosive passage of transition takes off like a shot. The music is loud and forceful, with rushing strings and plenty of horns, trumpets, and drums. Propelling the music along is a four-note rhythm exactly the same as the one found in Beethoven's Fifth Symphony. Moreover, because the cadence motive also began with repeated notes, you may feel an ongoing connection between these similarly constructed rhythmic figures and the first subject, but don't worry if you don't find this point obvious. It will become so, very shortly. Note that the music of this transition lacks thematic interest: it's all rhythmic energy, and I am sure that you will have no problem understanding why I call episodes such as this "motion music." The feeling of "going somewhere" couldn't be stronger.

Second Subject (at 1:38)
The motion music rapidly reaches a climax and stops abruptly, as a solo flute introduces the second subject. Contrary to everything heard so far, this is a lovely, perfectly symmetrical tune of great purity and innocence. It has two evenly balanced phrases, both beginning with the same music and each sweetly lyrical, flowing, and singable—a single thought, as opposed to the first subject's three distinct sections. This tune is repeated by a solo oboe, and the very light accompaniment includes an old friend: the seven-note squiggle from the first subject. There is no expressive significance to this practice. It's simply another way to tie everything together as part of one big musical paragraph. What gives this melody additional radiance is the fact that its phrases climb upwards, whereas every other idea in the movement (the plonks, the squiggles, the shout, and the cadence motive) moves downwards—even those two- and three-note sighs from the introduction.

Just look at the variety Haydn has already built into the two main subjects of his exposition, aside from placing them in their respective keys:

First Subject	Second Subject
three characters (cadence, squiggle, shout)	one character (single tune)
strings, oboes, full orchestra	solo flute, solo oboe
tiny motives	long, lyrical melody
development of introduction	totally new material
descending phrases	rising phrases
asymmetrical phrases	symmetrical phrases

Motion Music (at 1:56)

More motion music interrupts the melody of the second subject: a seesawing whirlwind of strings that accumulates energy as it goes, leading to a succession of six-repeated-note fanfares on the brass and woodwinds. Six repeated notes? Sure enough, the cadence motive from the first subject interjects hopefully, yet again trying to draw the music to a close, but the previous motion music chimes in with its four-note rhythm, and then the orchestra gradually thins out until the only thing left is a line of repeated notes in the violins over which the woodwinds emit a quizzical first-subject squiggle, seeming to say, "What on earth will happen next?" or something similar (as long as it has seven syllables). Once again development has happened even before the arrival of the formally designated section, and it has permitted Haydn to create an exposition that strikes the listener as a big, unified paragraph rather than a series of disconnected episodes—despite all the contrast built into it.

Exposition Repeat (at 2:36)

I noted in the discussion of repeats in general that Haydn often takes advantage of the existence of a large sectional return to design his themes in the knowledge that these will occur. In this case, ending the exposition with a steady rhythm of repeated notes and having a first subject that begins the same way means two things. First, the music can either go back to the beginning or forward into the development; and second, there's no way to predict in advance which of these events will happen—and when. Haydn in these situations invariably plans either option in a way that creates the maximum amount of surprise and suspense.

Development (at 4:15)

The following list of events suggests some of the expressive variety that Haydn wrings from the material of his exposition. These are my own personal impressions (yours may well be different) of the goings-on in the formal development section:

First Subject (at 4:15)
The repeated notes that ended the exposition continue, and under them, the two squiggles from the first subject engage in a sneaky conspiracy on bassoons and lower strings, like two thieves on tiptoe.

Motion Music (at 4:23)
Panic breaks out as the four-note rhythm stomps through the orchestra in anxious minor keys. Notice how this motive, formerly energetic but emotionally neutral, now sounds genuinely alarming.

Second Subject (at 4:32)
Whoops! False alarm: the second subject sails in, on solo flute followed by oboe exactly as in the exposition, its innocent lyricism more pronounced then ever and enhanced by the fact that Haydn changes practically nothing (only the accompaniment is a little bit more fully fleshed out this time around).

First Subject (at 4:56)
A loud interruption based on the end of the second subject introduces the cadence motive. It piles up angrily through the entire orchestra in the form of a loud argument that gets so confused that . . .

Motion Music (at 5:06)
. . . the six repeated notes of the cadence motive morph into the four-note rhythm of the motion music, reaching a natural climax that at the same time demonstrates (as promised) that the latter really does in fact derive from the former. This storm ends as did the exposition, in the form of an ongoing stream of repeated notes in the violins, only this time the strings progressively lose

steam, like a runner with barely enough energy left to get across the finish line.

It's worth mentioning that Haydn achieves all of this in exactly sixty-five seconds. The coldly analytical word *development* seems to me inappropriate for such an action-packed sequence of musical events.

Recapitulation (at 5:22)

As previously defined, the entire point of the recapitulation lies in reestablishing the home key, and this will necessarily involve a certain amount of recomposition. What Haydn does here is simply marvelous. The development section just barely manages to reintroduce the cadence motive—maybe now the ending has finally arrived? No way. Haydn achieves the necessary feeling of "staying home" by a simultaneous process of expansion and compression. If this sounds paradoxical, it really isn't. Listen to how he stretches out the soft–soft–loud sequence at 5:27 and then simply omits the motion music entirely, substituting instead a breezy, lyrical extension of the cadence motive in the strings. This leads directly to the second subject, first on solo oboe, and then more beautiful than ever as sung out by the full string section to a gorgeously enriched accompaniment of high horns (a Haydn specialty in C major) alternating with quiet trumpets and timpani.

So Haydn manages to have his cake and eat it too: the expanded first subject permits the music to continue growing and changing even beyond the development section, while the musical short-cut to the second subject that results ties the entire paragraph together as a single unit even more firmly than before. There's one additional subtlety worth pointing out. The extension of the cadence motive occurs as a series of rising phrases—in other words, almost as if it had been infected by some aspect of the second subject. This isn't a point that Haydn expects you to notice consciously, but it's one of those little touches that may strike you after living with the music for a while, and it contributes, however minutely, to the recapitulation's general aura of stability, of "being home." Great composers are always attentive to this sort of detail.

The second subject leads, as previously, to the whirlwind in the strings, and this time it's so energetic that even the cadence motive acquires a certain spastic enthusiasm (at 6:26): instead of six repeated notes, it apes the rhythm of the rushing strings—yet another example of the binding technique just described. For the last time, the motion music returns, only now a humorous coda intervenes. The cadence motive appears yet again in its quiet original form, as if to say, "This must *finally* be the end." But of course it's not: the orchestra repeats the cadence's last few notes, the violins toss in one last squiggle (almost identical in shape to the last bit of the second subject), and it's the shout that has the closing word. So a movement whose allegro section began with an ending actually ends, soft–soft–loud, with its first subject's middle, which is also (if you recall the introduction) the symphony's true beginning!

Now that I have described this movement in such excruciating detail, you may well be asking yourself if you are actually supposed to get all this the first couple of times listening, and the answer is, "Absolutely not." Descriptions of this sort have their risks. After all, what could fall flatter than a lengthy verbal discourse about an ongoing joke such as the one Haydn plays on his cadence motive? Either you get the punch line or you don't. However, I believe it's important to hear just how much content Haydn crams into this relatively brief span of time. The length of the movement doesn't begin to suggest the abundance of enjoyable and expressive moments that it offers.

With respect to the actual form, the various actors in this minidrama are all so clearly characterized that there's no possibility of mistaking them whenever they appear. As noted in my initial discussion of the sonata concept, the real challenge does not lie in creating highly differentiated themes and motives but in achieving a logically related, inevitable sequence of events—in finding unity within diversity, even if it strikes the listener primarily subconsciously. This is what I mean when I say that sonata forms engage your attention on two levels, the *expressive* (or emotional) and the *structural* (or intellectual). Just how intently you wish to listen remains a matter of personal choice, but the musical substance is always there regardless.

Example 2
String Quartet in F Major, Op. 74, No. 2 (1793)

First movement: Allegro spirituoso (CD 2, Track 1)

I chose this next example for several reasons: It was composed about the same time as Symphony No. 90 and so comes from roughly the same period in Haydn's life. This means that his treatment of form will be consistent with his compositional style from the late 1780s and early 1790s (I won't use the word mature, since Haydn's music was for all intents and purposes mature by about 1765). Both movements also have introductions thematically linked to their main bodies. The following table makes comparison of the two works easier:

Comparison of First Movements (in seconds)

	Symphony No. 90	String Quartet in F
Introduction	54	10
Exposition	102	90
Development	65	70
Recapitulation/Coda	91	84

First, note that the introductions are very different in length and also (it turns out) speed. That of the symphony is an adagio, while the quartet begins in the main allegro tempo. This gives Haydn room to write proportionally larger expositions, developments, and recapitulations in the chamber work (despite the slightly shorter length of the quartet movement overall). In both cases, you can see that the recapitulation is condensed as compared to the exposition and, it turns out, for the same reason. Because the themes are going to remain in the tonic, Haydn can drop some of the transitional motion music between what were originally his two principal key areas.

Logic would also dictate that since the quartet has a longer development, it should contain an even greater variety of ideas in its first and second subjects, right? Wrong. This first movement is what's called *monothematic,* one of Haydn's big formal innovations and a particularly misleading notion, because it suggests that the composer restricts himself to a single tune (or theme), which is hardly ever actually the case. In reality, what this means is a process in which the second subject derives largely from the first, always keeping in mind that in sonata form, there are no limits to the number of melodies, motives, or ideas that constitute a musical subject. So a movement that is technically monothematic may in fact employ a wider range of material than one that is not; it just adopts a different pattern of distribution.

There are two main reasons for this musical front-loading in Haydn. First, the real purpose of the second subject in a sonata movement is not so much to introduce new themes but rather to confirm the feeling of arrival at a different place, or key, distinct from the one in which the music started. Second, Haydn's music is so naturally developmental that by the time he reaches this new destination, he has often already created whole families of tunes and motives, giving the music all the forward impetus and contrast that it needs. In other words, Haydn's first subjects are so richly inventive that he may decide to construct (*evolve* is probably the more accurate term) the second subject from existing elements. This has the dual advantage of establishing the new tonality while binding together the entire exposition in one organic, continuous paragraph. It also saves time, leaving more space for development without making the piece seem overlong. This quartet offers a classic example of monothematicism. Here is the first movement's outline:

Introduction

Exposition (at 0:11)

Exposition repeated (at 1:40)

Development (at 3:10)

Recapitulation (at 4:20)

Coda (at 5:35)

Once again, I recommend that you listen a few times before reading on for a closer look. It's important to form your own impressions of how the music speaks to you, because in the final analysis, this is the reason you are going to listen to it in the first place, and your own reactions are just as valid as anyone's.

Introduction
Exposition (10 seconds later)

I lump the introduction and exposition together because the introduction consists of an extremely brief tune in the same tempo as the allegro proper. This tune, announced by the entire quartet in unison octaves, is a sort of primal outline of the true principal theme; or you might say that the first subject is a variation of the introduction. Either view is true to the facts. Making matters even more interesting, after the introduction, Haydn offers two versions of this tune, the first sweetly lyrical and folklike (quietly), the second urgently passionate and romantic, in a surging minor key (loudly). These are separated by pauses just like the one immediately following the introduction. So what you initially hear is: introduction (pause), theme—version one (pause), theme—version two.

From this opening, there's no way of knowing that the introduction is an introduction at all, and there's a good reason for this that I will mention in a moment. For the time being, pay attention to the fact that, even more than in the symphony, this play of melodic variations on the introduction creates the strongest possible impression of development and forward motion already in progress, even within the first half-minute of music. Given this fact, it makes no sense at all to worry about "first subjects" and "second subjects." The exposition basically consists of this opening theme separated by lyrical developments of its various rhythmic components and phrases. You can hear the opening theme return (and particularly its five-note beginning) at 0:58 and 1:28. The most striking contrasting element in the second subject is a lively dialogue between lower and upper strings (at 1:08), which is in turn related to the vigorous end of the introduction.

Another important contrasting element as the exposition proceeds is a typically Haydnesque gesture, in this case a very imaginative use of trills. You first encounter them in the motion music on the way to the second subject at 0:48. As the exposition draws to a close, the first violin has a further series of trills at 1:24, and finally the entire quartet goes crazy in a truly lunatic final cadence at 1:32. Haydn is in fact so adept at transforming the elements of his theme into distinct subsidiary ideas and presenting these in constantly changing textures that you may not even be conscious of the monothematic basis of this exposition, which is, to be frank, more or less the idea. Also, unlike the symphony, the motion music sounds highly lyrical and tuneful, which makes sense in a chamber work written entirely for melody instruments.

Besides, the real surprise comes at the end of the exposition, where once again it becomes clear that (as in the symphony) Haydn has special plans for the expected repeat. After a pause, two mysterious, long notes lead back to the beginning, which is not the introduction at all but the folk-music version of the principal theme. So in other words, it's only when the repeat happens that we learn that the opening tune was in fact an introduction and not the first subject. Furthermore, because the music seems to return to the middle of the opening and not its beginning, you may be forgiven for assuming that the development is beginning instead. It's only when the romantic version of the theme bursts in, exactly as originally, that it becomes clear that this is in fact a repeat and not something new. The effect may be compared to waking up in what appear to be unfamiliar surroundings, only to recognize the room and remember where you are a moment later. It's delightfully disorienting.

Development (at 3:10)

The opening of this section also consists of a pause, followed again by those two mysterious, long notes introducing the folk-music version of the main theme. It seems to lead back to the beginning once again. This time, however, a vast polyphonic development begins, taking the theme into anxious minor keys and generating an extraordinary level of tension. String-quartet writing, with its potential equality of balance between the four instruments, is naturally contrapuntal—that is, it lends itself very easily to passages in which the four players have simultaneous but independent musical lines (*polyphony*). The effect of counterpoint is the very opposite of musical drama (a sequence of related events moving in time). Rather, its effect is rhetorical, like a discussion or argument, but as you can hear, this also finds a natural place within the narrative structure that is sonata form.

This first argument comes to a full close, followed again by a pause (at 3:38). Haydn is, by the way, an acknowledged master in the dramatic use of silence to create suspense. After the pause, Haydn launches the romantic version of the main theme (quietly this time), leading to the suspicion, given all that has happened before, that perhaps the recapitulation has already begun, once again in the middle—recall the similar case of the exposition repeat. Instead, the development continues with a fresh argument, even more intense and passionate than the previous one. This rises to a huge climax, culminating in a surprising return to the final bars of the introduction (at 4:12). Another pause, and we naturally expect the folk-music version of the theme to begin the recapitulation, as happened at the opening of the quartet.

Recapitulation (at 4:20)

But no! A new, mysterious two-note lead-in precedes the principal theme, making the beginning of the recapitulation sound just like the opening of the development section. Once again, it's only when the romantic version of the tune strikes up that Haydn confirms that the music is indeed where it ought to be. He has now presented this theme in one of its original forms no less than five times, always in a way that sounds totally fresh and unexpected, nowhere more so than when he is in fact repeating it literally. A lesser composer writing a monothematic movement such as this might avoid repeating his main theme so often, but Haydn positively revels in it. Having the opportunity to hear the main theme frequently but without it ever turning stale means that the course of the music will be far easier to follow, and as the development shows, this frees Haydn to push the material to emotional extremes without having to worry about losing his listeners.

As in the symphony, the music operates at two levels: you can certainly enjoy the contrast between the various versions of the

theme, the motion music, and the emotionally turbulent development, but Haydn also invites you to relish each presentation of the
melody as a surprising event within the context of the movement
as a whole. And note how simply he accomplishes this, merely
by artful placement of those mysterious, two-note lead-ins and
careful selection of what actually gets repeated. The very end of
the movement (at 5:35) contains one last treat in the form of a
concluding, emphatic return to the introduction (slightly varied
to emphasize the feeling of finality). It would be difficult to imagine a more cogent or effective closing gesture.

Haydn's technique in this movement is so unlike what he does
in the symphony that you might well question how two such
differently imagined pieces could both fall under the umbrella of
sonata form. If in the orchestral work the principal challenge lay
in finding unity within diversity, then in the quartet it was just
the opposite: creating diversity out of unity through variations on
the first movement's single principal theme. In both cases, however, the overriding goal is the same: coherence without stiffness,
a natural spontaneity that avoids turning episodic, beauty that
never cloys, and a just balance between feeling (understanding
what the music says) and intellect (enjoyment of how the music
says it). Haydn's works are the sports cars of classical music: the
design of the vehicle is as sleek and hot as the ride is exciting.

This, then, is the sonata ideal: structure and content comple-
ment each other and coexist in perfect harmony, imbuing each
piece with its own special character while at the same time
defining the composer's personal sound and idiom. In these
two examples, you have heard a broad range of themes—witty,
catchy, expressive, and very memorable—but only one of them
could realistically be called a "song tune." This is because in the
sonata style, formal variety depends on the composer's ability
to come up with new and original kinds of themes and musical
materials. The fact that no two sonata-form movements by Haydn

are exactly the same speaks volumes about his inexhaustible fund of inspiration, but it also makes him impossible to predict. This need to expect the unexpected may not have helped his posthumous popularity, but as you can hear for yourself, it's where the fun really begins.

How to Listen
to Complete Works

*Haydn always planned his compositions whole. . . . His scores
are neat and clearly notated, and seldom contain corrections.
"This is because I do not write until I feel certain of how the
piece should go," he explained.*

—G. A. Griesinger

In this chapter, I am going to guide you through an entire
Haydn symphony—No. 88, my musical best friend—with
an ear to hearing how the techniques of narrative, dramatic
surprise, action, and reaction apply to all its movements, and
also how these concepts turn four highly differentiated sections
into a coherent, satisfying, and colorful whole. This last point is
a bit controversial. One of the most obvious methods of binding
a large work together—the sharing of entire themes between
movements—is almost never found in classical-period works,
although it is very characteristic of much later romantic music.
There's a very sensible reason for this. Most multimovement
pieces written in the classical period are short enough and suf-
ficiently tightly organized so as not to need this particular kind
of help. Big, long, more loosely structured romantic symphonies
and chamber works often do need it.

Furthermore, if (as discussed in the previous chapter) Haydn's
forms really do vary according to the nature of his ideas, then

nothing could be more disruptive to the music's structural integrity than the sudden intrusion into one movement of material specifically tailored to another. He would be buying long-term unity at the expense of internal coherence within each section, and that represents an unacceptable and unnecessary compromise. The proof of this is the finale of Symphony No. 46, where the minuet shows up in the middle of the finale and throws the movement into such alarmingly funny confusion that it just barely manages to cross the finish line. Aside from this singular exception, which is a deliberate joke, the truth is that Haydn's music is full of elements that can be used to bind one movement to the next and create a satisfying impression of an organic, large-scale design.

So here goes:

Symphony No. 88 in G Major (1787) (CD 1, Tracks 1–4)

*Scoring: 1 flute, 2 oboes, 2 bassoons, 2 horns, 2 trumpets,
          timpani, and strings*
1. Adagio (3/4)—Allegro (2/4)
2. Largo (3/4)
3. Menuetto: Allegretto (3/4)
4. Allegro con spirito (2/4)

As suggested previously, if you have time, try to listen to the entire symphony before reading the following description. This will give you a chance to form your own impressions, and knowing what the music sounds like in general will also make the following discussion more immediately useful. As a clue to the work's expressive content, if you know your Beethoven symphonies, you will be on firm ground here, for the melodies themselves live very much in the world of the Sixth "Pastoral" Symphony, while the music's formal shapes, sonic panorama, and sheer gusto recall the Seventh. Although this piece was composed about two decades earlier than the two Beethoven works, you may well find the comparisons both apt and enlightening.

I. Adagio—Allegro (Track I)

I included the time signatures in the complete list of movements because they reveal some potentially useful information. In a sense this is cheating: you often can't tell for sure, when listening, what precise rhythm a piece employs, nor is the above organization in any way standard. Still, you can certainly hear the basic distinction between *duple* (march) and *triple* (waltz/dance) meters in close proximity, and also feel the rhythmic similarities between movements that share the same time signatures. So just keep this information in the back of your mind for now.

The adagio introduction belongs not just to the first movement but to the whole symphony, even though it is melodically self-contained and (unlike the case of Symphony No. 90) shares not a single theme with any other movement or section. It does, however, contain several tiny motives or gestures that turn out to be quite important. Consider the logic of binding together a large work using small, simple components. It saves time because it does not require the wholesale repetition of themes from one movement to the next, but it still permits the composer to incorporate these often very memorable fragments into the actual melodic and motivic material of the work, as the requirements of large-scale continuity demand.

In this case, the significant elements worth remembering are

- the grandly declamatory opening, in which bold pronouncements for the full orchestra (minus trumpets and drums) in jagged rhythms alternate with quiet, pleading responses in the strings;
- the smoothly flowing sequence that brings the introduction to its close, containing a figure of four notes in even rhythm, punctuated by a rapid oscillation or melodic "turn."

In addition, this introduction gives the music a sense of solemnity and formality that the playful opening of the ensuing allegro couldn't possibly suggest on its own. If you have any doubts on this point, then try this experiment: Cue your CD player up to 1:10 of track 1 and start the symphony with its principal theme, leaving out the introduction entirely. If that doesn't convince you, then nothing will.

Haydn, particularly in his late instrumental works, often wrote slow introductions to his opening quick movements, and it is one of many elements that Beethoven adapted to his own purposes. His Seventh Symphony also begins with a slow introduction, on a much larger scale than Haydn's, but the principal is the same. The theme of Beethoven's allegro would sound just as out of place beginning the symphony straight away as Haydn's does. This, then, represents the first of many points of contact between the two works, and as with all such comparisons, the point is not to prove that one is better than the other because it did something "first" but rather to emphasize that similar musical problems often result in similar solutions, albeit each in the composer's own personal style.

As in the String Quartet Op. 74, No. 2, discussed in the last chapter, as well as the first movement of Beethoven's Seventh, this particular opening allegro is monothematic; virtually everything that happens in it derives from the first subject. Given its importance, it pays to listen carefully: the opening tune consists of four brief motives, three of which have an identical rhythm of seven notes divided into groups of four plus three. The fourth and last motive is a cadence: it brings the melody to a close. As played initially by first and second violins with its opening three notes harmonized in fifths (like the drone of a bagpipe), this melody has a certain folklike, pastoral quality very characteristic of the symphony as a whole (and the first movement of Beethoven's

Sixth). It's also extremely catchy and short. Once it gets into your head, it stays.

Often in works of the classical and romantic periods, the initial statement of a theme will be followed immediately by a repetition, technically called a *counterstatement*. If the melody first appears softly, the counterstatement will usually be loud, and vice versa. Haydn's counterstatement (at 1:18) shows once again that the music begins developing immediately, for it does more than repeat the tune. It also introduces a very important new accompaniment motive in the lower strings and bassoons. This vigorous oscillation, ending with an abrupt upward thrust, may bring to mind the end of the introduction. The motion music further confirms this link, because its primary driving force is the first four notes of the principal theme, which Haydn detaches for this purpose (at 1:37). So: four notes in even rhythm and a little oscillation or melodic turn—both are conspicuous elements highlighted at the end of the introduction, and out of them Haydn constructs his first subject.

The tiny second subject appears at 1:53, and one of the reasons it's so small stems from the fact that you can clearly hear its derivation from the opening theme (true also of Beethoven's Seventh). This means, practically speaking, that the largest part of the exposition consists neither of the first nor second subjects but of motion music, a joyous and breezy hubbub of activity in which Haydn demonstrates how just a few simple motives can be transformed into big, flowing, melodically generous sentences. Unlike what you heard in Symphony No. 90, the repeat of the exposition is not an opportunity for surprise. Just the opposite: it sounds extremely logical and "right," and so gives what is otherwise an unusually compact movement just the extra breadth that it needs.

The development, which begins at 3:57 with whispered reiterations of those tiny melodic turns from the introduction, finds every expressive possibility in the opening tune and its accompaniment motive. First it sounds softly anxious, then hesitant (at 4:01), then angry as melody and accompaniment reverse positions (at 4:23), until at last, after much further discussion, the motion music breaks in (at 4:57) and the development draws to a close very similar to the end of the exposition. So when the first subject returns (now with a flute warbling above, at 5:10), it has that same feeling of inevitability.

As happened in the two examples in the last chapter, the recapitulation is compressed, with an even shorter allusion to the already miniscule second subject, in this case to make room for a coda containing one last, brilliant statement of the opening theme. The final bars, with their bold exchanges between strings and winds, with horns especially prominent, carve up the first subject's seven-note motive more clearly than ever before into units of 4 + 3, showing once again that the music continues evolving right up to the final bar. The overall sonority of these closing measures, with prominent horns blaring out the main theme, once again seems to foretell the similar moment in the first movement of Beethoven's Seventh Symphony.

2. Largo (Track 2)

This largo is one of the most widely admired slow movements of its era. Brahms was blown away by it, and no wonder! Its exquisitely sculpted melody captures the very essence of delicate beauty. You might describe it as a very unusual set of variations, except that the whole point is that the tune itself hardly changes at all. In reality, the movement creates its own form. This isn't at all unusual in Haydn, and it's why, when listening, you shouldn't worry about the music fitting into predetermined patterns or structures, but simply take it as it comes. In this case, the sonata dialectic of action and reaction very much applies. The actual form of the movement, leaving aside the fact that virtually none of its repetitions is absolutely identical despite the fact that they pretend to be, looks like this: AAABAABABAB.

Like the opening theme of the first movement, the main tune (A) consists of four phrases, all rhythmically similar. The first two are identical, while the third phrase gets extended to close with a short cadence, and the fourth phrase is designed to lead back to the first—at least most of the time, because it comes in four different variants, and one of these reinforces the previously heard cadence. This may sound confusing, but it's really not when you hear it. All you need to know is that no matter what that fourth phrase does, this gorgeous melody either leads back to itself or gets interrupted by something else. The "form," then, is really nothing more than the tale of a tune so pretty that, like the Greek myth of Narcissus, it doesn't want to stop admiring its own reflection and so needs to be shaken up.

Haydn gives the melody to the unforgettable combination of solo oboe and solo cello (a Haydnesque fingerprint: the symphonies are full of important cello solos), while the rest of the orchestra provides a pastoral, Arcadian landscape, including gentle breezes in the violins (at 3:06) and birdcalls from the second oboe (at 4:37). It's all perfectly calculated to enhance the tune's gentle indolence, and like the principal theme of the first movement, the music has that indefinable, folkish quality characteristic of the entire work. Haydn presents the melody three times, enriching the accompaniment on each repetition while the actual tune remains the same, except for that fourth phrase. The first time (at 0:24), it leads directly back to the theme; the second time around, a melancholy minor-key extension wants to take the tune elsewhere (at 1:11) but doesn't succeed. After the third repetition, Haydn shortens the fourth phrase and brings it to a full close (at 1:45), as if to say, "Never mind. I give up."

The "shake-up," or B section, happens in the form of a shocking interruption from the full orchestra, with trumpets and timpani used for the very first time in the symphony. Haydn has kept them in reserve for this single moment of surprise, which is every bit as startling as anything in the "Surprise" Symphony (No. 94). Even more startling, what the full orchestra plays is nothing less than a loud, slowed-down version of the four-note motive of the first movement's opening theme. So now you can hear another reason why Haydn took such pains to make this bit of the tune independent and to boldly highlight it at the end of that movement. Furthermore, this loud interruption not only cuts off the main theme, it also alternates with a very quiet answer in the woodwinds, and these abrupt contrasts of loud and soft in slow tempo hark back to those declamatory exchanges from the introduction.

The loud outburst has no immediate effect on the tune, however, which sails in once again completely unruffled and manages yet another repeat, although the scoring is always slightly different on each of its reappearances. An even more violent interruption ensues, and this has an impact: the tune reacts (at 4:00) in a sorrowful variation. "Gotcha!" says a foreshortened version of B (at 4:24) in a series of two-note interjections. But no, the melody regains its composure and sails in yet again, with little chirping birdcalls on the second oboe providing the most deliciously colored accompaniment thus far. Note that although the tempo is quite slow, Haydn has structured the movement to increase the tension and pace of events as the music proceeds: three repetitions of A initially; then two; then a single, tense variation; then one last reprise.

The final repetition of the tune comes to a full close, but the four-note outburst actually has the last word. These two antithetical characters remain as they were at the beginning, their positions unchanged. Even though this movement can by no stretch of the imagination be considered to be in textbook sonata form, it certainly falls within the sonata style in its contrasts and the way its themes interact (or charmingly ignore each other). Beyond that, Haydn's way of building the main theme out of four rhythmically similar phrases, his employment of the first movement's four-note motive, and the pastoral atmosphere all define the music as belonging to a larger family, and suggest that it represents a step in an overall process that will only find its culmination in the symphony's finale.

3. Menuetto: Allegretto (Track 3)

Coming after the freeform, lyrical largo, the minuet offers a simple and strict design, as well as a clear emphasis on rhythm. Virtually all minuets have the same ABA structure. Each section has two halves, both of which are repeated at least the first time around (the final return of A may or may not include the repeats, depending on the performance). The B section is called a *trio* for reasons that in Haydn's day no longer had anything to do with the number three. So as you hear it, and with numbers standing for each half-section, most classical examples of this dance type sound like this: minuet: (A1)(A1)(A2)(A2)—trio: (B1)(B1)(B2)(B2)—minuet: (A1)(A2).

Minuets typically have strong associations with powdered wigs and aristocratic court balls, but many of Haydn's proudly reveal strong peasant roots, and this one may well be his most folklike of all, with a hearty vigor that fits perfectly into everything heard so far. Even more remarkable, the main theme (A1) transforms virtually all the shared characteristics previously described. As is the case with the first two movements, it contains four short phrases, each rhythmically similar (the first three are identical, the fourth is extended). Each phrase begins with a melodic-turn upbeat (remember the introduction), followed by four notes in even rhythm reinforced by the timpani.

Now it's clear why Haydn ended the largo the way he did, with trumpets and drums pounding out exactly the same four-note motive in the slow tempo. Furthermore, the first and fourth phrases of the minuet's opening tune bear a striking resemblance to their counterparts in the largo (and now you may recall that both movements use the same meter as well). Compare, for example, 0:24 in the largo to 0:09 in the minuet, or better still, simply memorize the first phrase (it's only five notes) of the slow movement's melody and hum it in the faster tempo. You'll hear the resemblance immediately.

This raises an interesting issue that most commentators, committed to musical analysis of the printed score, miss. It might be pushing it to claim that the theme of this minuet is an actual variation of the largo's tune in a strict or academic sense. But for the purposes of establishing a feeling of unity, of relatedness, it isn't necessary for the music to pass some preexisting analytical hurdle. All the composer has to do is *suggest* a resemblance in a way that the audience will catch when listening, and this only requires a couple of notes, a distinctive rhythm or harmony, or any of these in combination. Everything else can be completely different, and often will be.

The entire A section basically consists of these melodic-turn upbeats followed by four-note phrases, but its second half once again shows the sonata principle at work, for it contains a short development section that leads back to a literal reprise of the opening theme. This is what distinguishes a stylized, symphonic minuet such as this one from a real dance number. The development section (that is, A2) begins at 0:38 and spends most of its time in dialogue between the orchestra's high and low instruments, vigorously playing with the rhythm of those turn-plus-four-note phrases. It quickly works back to the opening theme (at 1:02), which brings the A section to a robust close.

As I mentioned in the introduction to this book, the trio (or B section) got me hooked on classical music when I was very young. It consists of pure tone painting, an evocative rural scene with bagpipe or hurdy-gurdy drones and lazy, irregularly phrased melodies soaring above. Haydn even touches in those memorable, chirping birdcalls from the largo: compare 4:37 from the second movement to 2:08 and 2:43 in the trio. This is yet another detail instantly vivid when listening but completely lost when studying the score because of the differences between the two movements in scoring, tempo, and notation. The relationship is nonetheless unmistakable, and in the trio, Haydn makes his intentions extra clear by isolating these figures with syncopated accents and a touch of harmonic spice as well.

It's impossible to capture the color and feel of this music in words: it opens a view onto an imaginary, idyllic world, perhaps another vision of the Arcadian landscape that Haydn conjured up in the largo, and there is nothing else in the symphonic literature that sounds quite like it. Its rustic, outdoors quality does, however, find an interesting counterpart in the trio of the scherzo of Beethoven's Seventh Symphony and the country-dance third movement of the Sixth. The return of the A section concludes a movement that for all its evident formal simplicity has a lot to say, combining earthiness and sophistication effortlessly.

4. Allegro con spirito (Track 4)

In the first movement, Haydn used monothematic sonata form. Here, also in 2/4 time, he writes a monothematic rondo. This may appear something of a paradox, and it is, at least to the extent that a rondo usually has the form ABACA. In other words, it consists of a principal tune (the *ritornello*) separated by episodes based on different material. Haydn never saw any point in introducing new themes when he could still use an existing one, not because he was at a loss for ideas or simply being cheap, but because for him, transforming a single theme from happy to sad or from calm to angry was the best way to obtain maximum expressiveness within the unfolding of the musical narrative. In other words, he doesn't abandon his characters midstory.

He has also designed a rondo subject that not only is one of the catchiest and most unforgettable tunes in the history of music, it also derives pretty obviously from the main theme of the first movement and, in particular, from the version that becomes its brief second subject. Compare the beginning of this finale to the passage at 1:59 in the opening movement. There are other resemblances here as well, such as the three-note rhythm that hesitantly closes the first part of the first movement's development section (at 4:13). This same idea, now strong and vigorous, performs exactly the same function in concluding the first episode of the finale (at 1:39).

Most importantly, though, Haydn has designed his ritornello as a sort of apotheosis of all the tunes heard so far. The tune has two halves, both repeated on its first appearance (afterwards it's played straight through). Its first half consists—you guessed it— of four phrases containing four notes in even rhythm followed by a melodic turn. In other words, it's the minuet pattern (turn then four-note rhythm) only played backwards and much faster. The full theme without repeats contains sixteen repetitions (that is, four times four) of this basic motive, and has the shape A (four reps) B (8 reps) A (4 reps), and so it reflects in its own shape the fundamental structural principle of the rondo itself, which is simply a departure from and return to the opening tune. Many of Haydn's rondo themes have a similar outline, however different the actual melodies or their rhythmic and motivic constituents. This particular example, a veritable orgy of the number four, thus summarizes the musical content of the whole symphony.

The first episode (at 0:56) begins with motion music, just as the first movement did after playing its principle tune, and this leads (at 1:14) to a varied statement of the ritornello theme in a pensive minor key. The procedure is very similar to the arrival of the second subject three movements previously, so up through its B episode, this rondo actually resembles the first movement's exposition. The return of the main theme (at 1:42) might even be mistaken for an exposition repeat, but its second A section turns into a whole new episode (at 2:04). In a virtuoso display of counterpoint, a three-part *canon* (that is, a round in which each part plays the same music in staggered entries) begins a vigorous chase through the orchestra, coming to a close in a stern minor key. The canon functions almost like a development section, and so between its two episodes this movement also has a strong whiff of the sonata principle, despite being ostensibly in a lighter and more episodic form—sonata disguised as a rondo.

The mischievous, whispered lead-back is Haydn at his most sly. He toys with the four-note motive as well as the listener's expectations as to when the ritornello will actually reappear. After one more time through the tune (its chugging accompaniment very amusingly enriched by horns and bassoons), the orchestra pulls up short with a few abrupt chords and then races off in a thrilling coda, whose energy and brilliant writing for high horns once again points forward to the similar conclusion of Beethoven's Seventh. The closing gesture, three repeated chords, is a musical fingerprint fairly typical of these late symphonies. In a bit less then four minutes, Haydn has summarized the entire content of the work—a sort of musical day in the countryside—not just in the structure and design of its themes, but also in distilling the essence of their rustic folk character, good humor, and obstinate memorability.

So catchy is the tune of this rondo, in fact, that you might perhaps think it's too popular, too frivolous, to conclude a supposedly serious piece such as a symphony. It's worth pointing out, then, that the main issue with any finale in a classical-period symphony is not how grand it is but how well it fits—whether it is the "right" finale. You have already heard that Haydn took pains to make the opening movement unusually light and genial in order to maximize its friendly, folklike character. The biggest movement in this particular symphony, in terms of both contrast and range of expression, is the largo. Moreover, the two related inner movements, even though they are simpler in form, together create a more imposing block than the two related outer ones, and this too enhances the symphony's pastoral credentials. You will find exactly the same strategy at work in Beethoven's Sixth Symphony, in which the deliberately naïve opening acts as a prelude to the more ample "Scene by the Brook," while the finale provides a gentle but still fulfilling conclusion after the combined scherzo and thunderstorm.

In sum, the distribution of weight among the movements in any sonata-style work, like the forms themselves, is the natural result of what the music wants to express, and not a foregone conclusion. Despite the fact that most symphonies will have four movements arranged in the pattern fast–slow–dance–fast, there are no rules as to which of these movements must be the most significant, the longest, or the most highly developed. All that matters is that the sequence of feelings and moods, the pattern of tension and relaxation, should make logical and emotional sense and leave you satisfied when the piece comes to its close.

This means that in considering the 88th Symphony as a whole, both the relative balance between its movements and the interior relationships that Haydn creates are unique to this work. Many Haydn symphonies, for example, contain themes based on the repetition of rhythmically identical motives, even a fourfold repetition, but no other symphony turns this innocent fact into a binding principal that unites all its various parts to quite this degree. Used once, it's a brilliant stroke of genius. Used twice or three times, it becomes a formula, then ultimately a cliché, tired and predictable. And so whatever the resemblances to other works, whether melodic or structural, you will only find this particular technique, treated in this particular way, in this particular symphony.

Here is a summary of the various elements at work linking up the symphony's movements and where you have heard them:

	Movements
Loud statements, quiet answers	1, 2
Four notes in even rhythm	1, 2, 3, 4
Bird chirps	2, 3
Bagpipe fifths	1, 3
Main theme in four similar phrases	1, 2, 3, 4
The oscillation, or "turn"	1, 3, 4
Melodic similarities	(2, 3) and (1, 4)
Formal correspondences	4 mirrors 1
The sonata principle (not "the form")	1, 2, 3, 4

Notice that none of these require that you know the time signatures mentioned at the beginning of this discussion, still less have any conscious view of Haydn's long-term treatment of key and tonality, which basically takes care of itself. And the list is by no means exhaustive; you may well have heard things that I didn't. There is no single, correct answer. If you heard it, then it exists, and that's all there is to it. Listeners have the choice of approaching the music from many different angles, any one of which offers a full measure of satisfaction all by itself.

Haydn in His Own Words

It would be very interesting to know what inspired Haydn to write his compositions, and also the feelings and ideas that he had in mind and tried to express in his own musical idiom. To discover this specifically, however, it would have been necessary to review with him one work after another, and that annoyed the old man. But he did admit that he frequently depicted moral characterizations in his symphonies.

—G. A. Griesinger

The relationship between life and art, even when the artist is unusually forthcoming and his life well documented, is always a tricky subject. This is particularly true of music, because the abstract nature of so much of it often begs for an explanation of what the composer really "means" or what the story is "behind" a given work. In such cases, the usual knee-jerk reaction is to turn to facile biographical explanations that often wind up trivializing the music when they don't distract attention away from it entirely. However, Haydn is so interesting a figure that a brief character sketch seems to be in order. Only here, I prefer to let the great man himself do most of the talking, in six letters and quotations.

1. I have been in the company of emperors, kings and many great men, and I received many flattering words from them: but I

have never desired to live on close terms with such people and prefer to be with my own kind.

2.   My prince was content with all of my efforts, and gave me his approval. As leader of the orchestra I could experiment, take note of what made an impression, and what lessened it, and so could improve by adding, trimming, and taking risks. I was isolated from the rest of the world. There was no one nearby to bother me or distract me from my chosen path, and so I was obliged to become original.

These are two of the most famous of all of Haydn's statements about himself and his work, quoted in virtually all of the biographical literature. He was a man who knew his place and felt comfortable in his own skin. This quiet confidence must have been a great help to him in his professional life. It's important to keep in mind that in his more than four decades of service to multiple princes of the Esterházy family (from 1766 until his death in 1809), Haydn was not only a composer; he was for much of that time in charge of a vast musical establishment that included the orchestra, an opera company, the church services, and all the chamber and ceremonial music that the household required for daily entertainment. Prince Nicholas was also an accomplished performer on the baryton, an obsolete cello-like instrument for which Haydn composed hundreds of assorted chamber pieces.

Although some of his new compositions technically belonged to the prince, at least for a limited period of time, it is easy to understand how Haydn's increasing international fame also served to enhance the status of his patron, and so reinforced the happy situation in which Haydn essentially had carte blanche to write just about anything he chose so long as it reflected well on house Esterházy. Haydn's originality, then, was not accidental or mysterious but self-willed and deliberate, the conscious act of a musical genius working under conditions virtually ideal for his artistic growth.

Perhaps no other composer in history had the benefit of such comprehensive, day-in, day-out, practical experience. The musicians and singers under Haydn's management were often among the finest in the Europe. Several were notably famous themselves, and practically all the most important composers of the younger generation (including Mozart and Beethoven) considered Haydn to be their teacher, either in fact or in spirit. He was, without a doubt, lucky in his situation, but there did come a time when the conflict between increasing international acclaim and life as a mere servant began to get on his nerves.

3. February 9, 1790

Nobly born,
Most highly respected and kindest Frau von Genzinger,

Well, here I sit in my wilderness—forsaken—like a poor waif—almost without any human society—melancholy—full of the memories of past glorious days—yes! Past alas!—and who knows when these days shall return again? Those wonderful parties? Where the whole circle is one heart, one soul—all these beautiful musical evenings—which can only be remembered, and not described—where are all these enthusiastic moments?—all gone—and gone for a long time. Your Grace mustn't be surprised that I haven't written up to now to thank you. I found everything at home in confusion, and for 3 days I didn't know if I was Capell-master or Capell-servant. Nothing could console me, my whole house was in confusion, my pianoforte which I usually love so much was perverse and disobedient, it irritated me rather then calmed me, I could only sleep very little, even my dreams persecuted me; and then, just when I was happily dreaming I was listening to the opera *Le nozze di Figaro*, that horrible North wind woke me and almost blew my nightcap off my head; I lost 20 lbs. in weight in 3 days, for

the good Viennese food I had in me disappeared on the journey; alas! Alas! I thought to myself as I was eating in the mess
here, instead of that delicious slice of beef, a chunk of a cow
50 years old; instead of a ragout with little dumplings, an old
sheep with carrots; instead of a Bohemian pheasant, a leathery
joint; instead of those fine and delicate oranges, a Dschable or
so-called gross Sallat [sic]; instead of pastry, dry apple-fritters
and hazelnuts—that's what I have to eat. Alas! Alas! I thought
to myself, if I could only have a little bit of what I couldn't
eat up in Vienna. —Here in Estoras no one asks me: Would
you like some chocolate, with milk or without? Will you take
some coffee, black, or with cream? What may I offer you, my
dear Haydn? Would you like a vanilla or a pineapple ice? If I
only had a good piece of Parmesan cheese, especially in Lent,
so that I could more easily swallow those black dumplings and
noodles; just today I told our porter here to send me a couple
of pounds. . . . (Landon 1978, 2:737)

This amusing letter touches on the fact that Haydn was a
"hands on" composer, who worked at the keyboard. It could
hardly have been otherwise. His musical ideas are so tactile, so
finely judged rhythmically, and so intimately tied to the experience of listening in real time that it should come as no surprise
to learn that he spent considerable time improvising at his piano,
honing specific details, and making sure that any spontaneous
discoveries and surprises carried over into the finished score.
But even more importantly, this letter introduces the one person
who meant more to Haydn, as both a friend and colleague, than
anyone else: Mozart. From the time that the younger composer
acknowledged Haydn as his "teacher" in dedicating to him six
magnificent string quartets in 1785, the two had become fast
friends. Haydn famously and without hesitation acknowledged
Mozart as "the greatest composer known to me," and he backed
up his words with deeds:

4.   To Franz Roth, Prague

December 1787

. . . You ask me for an opera buffa. Most willingly, if you want
to have one of my vocal compositions for yourself alone. But
if you intend to produce it on the stage at Prague, in that case
I cannot comply with your wish, because all of my operas are
far too closely connected with our personal circle (Esterház,
in Hungary), and moreover they would not produce the proper
effect, which I calculated in accordance with the locality. It
would be quite another matter if I were to have the great good
fortune to compose a brand new libretto for your theatre. But
even then I should be risking a good deal, for scarcely any man
can brook comparison with the great Mozart.

If I could only impress on the soul of every friend of music,
and on high personages in particular, how inimitable are
Mozart's works, how profound, how musically intelligent,
how extraordinarily sensitive! (for this is how I understand
them, how I feel them)—why then the nations would vie
with each other to possess such a jewel within their frontiers.
Prague should hold him fast—but should reward him, too; for
without this, the history of great geniuses is sad indeed, and
gives but little encouragement to posterity to further exertions;
and unfortunately this is why so many promising intellects fall
by the wayside. It enrages me to think that this incomparable
Mozart is not yet engaged by some imperial or royal court!
Forgive me if I lose my head: but I love the man so dearly.

I am, &c.

Joseph Haydn (Landon 1978, 2:702)

Haydn's total lack of professional jealousy—his almost fright-
eningly dispassionate view of his own abilities as well as those of
others and his willingness to simply step aside in favor of Mozart
in service to the cause of promoting great music—says something

very powerful about his motivations and his belief in himself and his mission. At the time, Haydn's fervent statements about Mozart (he also referred to him as "a god") would certainly have been considered eccentric, particularly coming from the mouth of the composer that the rest of the world regarded as "the god." History has subsequently vindicated Haydn's high opinion of his dearest friend, unfortunately to some degree at the expense of Haydn's own reputation.

Nevertheless, music is not a zero-sum game; one composer's excellence does not inevitably diminish another's. More to the point, no one, but no one, seems to have been at this period a more perceptive, lucid, unbiased, and self-aware critic than Haydn. If he kept writing symphonies, string quartets, and other works after his encounters with Mozart and Beethoven, it could only have been because he knew that he need fear nothing from the comparison. In this, as in so many of his other musical judgments, he was completely correct, and it's only reasonable to suggest that if historical hindsight grants Haydn unique perceptiveness when on the subject of Mozart, it should value similarly the tacit appraisal of his own abilities embodied in the works that he composed after their initial encounter.

Mozart died during Haydn's first London visit. The shock of receiving the news was evidently tremendous, and Haydn never fully got over it. He continued to stay on friendly terms with the family, continued to promote Mozart's music at every opportunity, and according to eyewitness testimony, could scarcely mention his friend's name in old age without bursting into tears.

Just a few months before Mozart's death, Haydn wrote the following letter from London to his mistress, the singer Luigia Polzelli.

5. To Luigia Polzelli, Vienna

August 4, 1791

Dear Polzelli!

I hope that you will have received my last letter through Count Fries and also the hundred florins [Gulden] which I transferred to you. I would like to do more, but at present I cannot. As far as your husband is concerned, I tell you that Providence has done well to liberate you from this heavy yoke, and for him, too, it is better to be in another world than to remain useless in this one. The poor man has suffered enough. Dear Polzelli, perhaps, perhaps the time will come, which we both so often dreamt of, when four eyes shall be closed. Two are closed, the other two—enough of all this, it shall be as God wills. Meanwhile, pay attention to your health. I beg of you, and write me very soon, because for quite some time now I have had days of depression without really knowing why, and your letters cheer me, even when they are sad. Good bye, dear Polzelli, the mail won't wait any longer. I kiss your family and remain always,

Your most sincere

Haydn (Landon 1978, 3:95–96)

This glimpse into Haydn's personal life is just too juicy to overlook. He was without question a ladies' man. He loved pretty women and flirted with them well into his old age. The sorry state of Haydn's marriage was well known to his friends and colleagues. As seems to happen with surprising frequency in the world of music—Mozart and Dvořák had similar experiences—he married the sister of his first love (she became a nun). Unlike those later cases, however, Haydn's union produced disastrous results. The couple had no children. Haydn's wife had no interest in music and seemed completely unaware of her husband's genius. It seems that no one had anything good to say about her.

For his part, Haydn referred to his wife as a "bigot" for spending too much time and money on the church, and he enjoyed the favors of several other women, both in London and on the continent. He was also evidently involved (as the letter shows) in a kind of informal competition with his wife to see which of them would outlive the other. While he was in London, his wife asked him to send money so that she could purchase a new house to occupy when she became a widow. Haydn didn't send the money but bought the place himself on his return. His wife died in 1800, nine years before he did.

6. To Jean Phillip Krüger on behalf of the members of the *Musikverein* in Bergen, on the Island of Rügen, North Germany

    22 September 1802

    Gentlemen,

    It was indeed a most pleasant surprise to receive such a flattering letter from a part of the world where I could never have imagined that the products of my poor talents were known. But when I see that not only is my name familiar to you, but my compositions are performed by you with approval and satisfaction, the warmest wishes of my heart are fulfilled: to be considered a not wholly unworthy priest of this sacred art by every nation where my works are known. You reassure me on this point as regards your fatherland, but even more, you happily persuade me—and this cannot fail to be a real source of consolation to me in my declining years—that I am often the enviable means by which you, and so many other families sensible of heartfelt emotion, derive, in their homely circle, their pleasure—their enjoyment. How reassuring this thought is to me!—Often, when struggling against the obstacles of every sort which oppose my labours: often, when the powers of mind and body weakened, and it was difficult for me to continue in the course I had entered on:——a secret voice whispered to me: 'There are so few happy and contented peoples here below; grief and sorrow are always their lot; perhaps your labours will once be a source from which the care-worn, or the man burdened with affairs, can derive a few moments' rest and refreshment.' This was indeed a powerful motive to press onwards, and this is why I now look back with cheerful satisfaction on the labours expended on this art, to which I have devoted so many long years of uninterrupted effort and exertion. And now I thank you in the fullness of my heart for your kindly thoughts of me, and beg you to forgive me for delaying my answer so long: enfeebled health, the inseparable companion of the grey-haired septuagenarian, and pressing business, deprived me till now of this pleasure. Perhaps nature may yet grant me the joy of composing a little memorial for you, from which you may gather the feelings of a gradually dying veteran, who, even after his death, would fain survive in the charming circle of which you draw so wonderful a picture. I have the honor to be, with profound respect.

Your wholly obedient servant,

Joseph Haydn (Landon 1978, 5:233)

This moving letter comes as close as any of Haydn's surviving statements to explaining his musical philosophy, and it describes in a single word the one quality that sums up his music best: "refreshment." In fact, I can't think of any other composer whose music is more innately refreshing than Haydn's. It makes you feel good, even when the emotions being expressed are anxious or sad. His unflagging energy, consummate technique, and unequalled sense of timing combine to create works whose unaffected warmth and vitality really do offer a very special depth of satisfaction and an escape from the sorrows and cares of the world.

Haydn's words also refute one more very damaging myth: the idea that his music was primarily written exclusively for a tiny minority of highly educated and sophisticated musical connoisseurs. Nothing could be further from the truth, and we have his own statement to prove it. To a certain extent, he rose to prominence by going over the heads of the critics and academics, and appealing directly to the music-loving public. This is only to be expected in a musician who, as a composer at least, had little formal education and was essentially self-taught. That said, Haydn was far too much of a craftsman ever to "write down" for the sake of popularity. He saw no reason why great music should not please everyone and contain a mix of elements specifically included to satisfy the widest range of tastes. His attitude resembles Shakespeare's, in that he prided himself on his ability to reach all strata of society. The better the music, the broader its appeal. This was his philosophy and goal from the very start, and it's worth keeping in mind as you listen to the music described in the following chapters.

Part 2

Movement Types in Haydn's Instrumental Music

Overview

Haydn occasionally mentioned that instead of the numerous quartets, sonatas, and symphonies, he should have written more vocal music. He might not just have found himself among the most famous opera composers of the day, but also setting music to a text is much easier than working without one.

—G. A. Griesinger

It's just one of those remarkable historical ironies that Haydn, superbly trained as a singer in the St. Stephens cathedral choir of Vienna, followed by several more years as apprentice/assistant to the renowned Italian singing teacher Porpora, ultimately became famous as a composer of instrumental music, whereas as Mozart, the great piano virtuoso of his age, wrote the first important operas in the modern repertoire and is arguably most highly acclaimed as a writer for the voice.

In the previous two chapters, I described Haydn's freedom of form and how the sonata principle applies to all the various parts of a large chamber or orchestral work. In fact, you may be relieved to know that the actual selection of movement types, whether in Haydn's day or our own, is not very large. Aside from sonata-form allegros, minuets (ABA), and rondos (ABACA, etc.), there are only a few other major options or variants, which follow:

1. Slow Movements

Song Form (ABA): This simple form is similar to that of a minuet, only the music is quite aptly more lyrical and may well feature an important instrumental solo, like a concerto (often in Haydn for flute, violin, cello, oboe, or horn).

Sonata Form: There are two kinds of sonata-form slow movements, one with, the other without, a development section. When the movement has a development section, its form will often sound indistinguishable from ABA—with B being the development—although the necessary disposition of keys and modulations, not to mention the possibilities for creating diverse first and second subjects, may well make the piece considerably longer than a nonsonata ABA. When the movement lacks a development section and has two clearly differentiated subjects, then its form will likely strike the listener as ABAB, with the reprise of both A and B almost invariably ornamented and enriched. Most of Haydn's early slow movements in all the instrumental genres in which he worked adopt one of these formal strategies.

2. Quick Movements

Sonata/Rondo: As discussed in connection with the finale of the 88th Symphony, Haydn soon began to fuse rondo and sonata forms together (as did Mozart). What this means in practical terms is that the first subject of the exposition returns in the home (tonic) key just before the development section, giving the music a rondo shape, and the recapitulation can then proceed in more or less normal order, with perhaps a final reappearance of the principal theme to close the basic, rondo form. There are many, many variants on this concept, however, and the important thing to keep

in mind is simply that the "feel" of such movements will generally be a touch more episodic (because of the regularly spaced
returns to the opening tune) than that of a plain sonata-form
quick movement. Haydn often signals "rondo" by the structure
of the principal theme: ABA, in two halves (that is A–BA), both
repeated at the start, as in the finale of Symphony No. 88.

Variation/Rondo: Haydn also enjoyed writing rondos in which
the reappearances of the ritornello theme are themselves
varied as the movement proceeds. I have included a sample (the
finale of Symphony No. 68) on CD 1, and will discuss it in its
appropriate place.

3. Variations (Both Slow and Quick)

Haydn was quite simply the greatest variation writer who ever
lived. Any composer who is committed to continuous development—and who avoids literal repetition to the degree that Haydn
does—had bloody well better be! As noted, even movements that
are not formally called variations, such as sonata-without-devel-
opment or certain types of rondo, can incorporate a very healthy
variation component. There are, however, many cases, mostly in
slow movements, where Haydn writes formal variation sets, and
you will hear several on the accompanying CDs.

In general, Haydn's variation movements come in two varieties, those written on a single theme and those written on two
themes that alternate, often in the process switching back and
forth from major to minor keys (or vice versa). This last type of
variation movement, a genuine Haydn original, turned out to be
critically important for later music, becoming the basis of the
great adagio in Beethoven's Ninth, as well as many of the most
famous slow movements by Bruckner, Mahler, and a host of other

composers. These alternating variation sets can be quite large. Haydn's magnificent and brooding Andante with Variations in F Minor for solo piano, at about a quarter of an hour's length, is as long as the corresponding movement in the Beethoven symphony and a perfectly satisfying, freestanding work on its own.

Aside from slow movements, Haydn may place variation sets anywhere: they can also open or conclude a work, and you will encounter them more often in the late pieces than in the earlier ones. Orchestral variations make particularly excellent platforms to showcase the abilities of various instrumental soloists. In a string quartet, each player may have a variation to himself, accompanied by the others. These are all opportunities that Haydn seized with particular enthusiasm.

4. Contrapuntal Forms (Fugue, Passacaglia)

Some of Haydn's most famous instrumental movements, particularly in the string quartets, are fugues, but you will also find them in the symphonies—if not always in strict form, then contained within a sonata structure in some way. A fugue is like a canon, or round, save that its principal theme (the subject) enters sequentially on different notes of the scale. Fugues are usually written for a fixed number of parts, or *voices,* and a complete statement of the subject in each voice is called an *exposition.* In between expositions the composer places *episodes,* and these can be very free in both style and content. A fugue exposition that leads to something else entirely (in other words, that isn't part of a strict fugue) is called a *fugato.*

A *passacaglia* is a set of free variations over a repeated bass line. The most famous example in orchestral music is probably the finale of Brahms's Fourth Symphony, and you will find many passacaglias in modern works by composers such as Benjamin

Britten and Dmitri Shostakovich. Haydn generally used this kind of writing as part of a larger variation-type structure in his chamber music. He composed no strict versions in the classic baroque sense of, say, Bach's famous Passacaglia and Fugue in C Minor for Organ, but within the more dynamic parameters of the sonata principle, every one of Haydn's examples is extraordinary. I have included samples of both fugue and passacaglia—in choral, chamber, and orchestral works—on the accompanying CDs.

Haydn was a "natural" at polyphonic writing. It came to him (or so it sounds) as easily as breathing. His contrapuntal movements and episodes fit organically into the scheme of contrast that he has designed for each individual movement or work. The effect such a texture has in the context of the dramatic sonata style can be understood in several ways: as that of a discussion between characters (ranging in mood from witty to angry), as a summing up after a period of intense activity (making an especially thoughtful finale), or as an extended meditation and moment of reflection on a single mood or feeling. It all depends on the expressive qualities of the melodies being used and where Haydn places them in his overall scheme of contrasts.

These, then, are the basic movement types that Haydn subsumed into the larger universe of the sonata principle. It is not a long list, nor are the forms themselves particularly complicated. In fact, their beauty lies in their fundamental simplicity and adaptability—as the next four chapters, in which I discuss all of the rest of the instrumental music on the two accompanying CDs, will show.

First Movements

Strict theoreticians...found a lot to criticize in Haydn's compositions, and they complained particularly about the debasement of music by means of comedy and joking. He was not disturbed, though, because he was certain that a strict application of the rules very often produced music lacking both taste and feeling—that many practices had without good reason assumed the authority of rules, and that in music the only thing that should be totally forbidden is something offensive to a discerning ear.

—G. A. Griesinger

In considering the sonata principle, you have already had the opportunity to hear three examples of first movements, from two symphonies and one quartet. They were all very different from each other, but this doesn't even begin to suggest the variety that Haydn was able to build into the basic classical sonata allegro. It's also worth mentioning that not all of Haydn's opening movements belong in this category. There are important works in all genres, for example, that begin with slow movements or variations. Still, the fact remains that the vast majority of first movements will be in some version of quick sonata form, and so I have selected three further pieces—also from two symphonies and one quartet—each of which differs completely from anything heard previously, both in expressive purpose and structural details. Taken together, these pieces explore the outer boundaries of mockery, anxiety, and lyric grace, and yet all of them achieve their impact thanks to the irresistible binding force of the sonata principle guided by the hand of its first true master.

Symphony No. 80 in D Minor (1784)

First Movement (CD 1, Track 6)
Scoring: flute, 2 oboes, 2 bassoons, 2 horns, strings

This zany opening movement, with its schizoid conflict between angst and triviality, stands so close to the world of Mahler conceptually that it's almost spooky. There is no point in worrying about first and second subjects here, because the essence of the exposition lies in its restless wavering between minor and major keys. This battle is present right at the start. The opening is grim and tense, and the first turn to the major (at 0:31) self-destructs with a wonderfully melodramatic shriek (at 0:41) that sends the music careening off in another direction entirely.

Shortly afterwards, just as the exposition comes bristling to its neurotic end, a tiny little closing theme chimes in, a trite hurdy-gurdy melody. Everything about this tune sounds wrong: its insolent mood, its waltz rhythm, and most of all, the seven-bar phrasing, which means that the theme always seems to end a measure sooner than it should. It's a wonderfully disorienting melody, and it also demonstrates why it is absolutely necessary to repeat the exposition: the return to the turbulent opening only heightens the bizarre contrast. Once again this corny tune brings the exposition to an end (at 2:45), and then—silence.

I noted in connection with the first movement of String Quartet Op. 74, No. 2, that Haydn is a master of timing, especially in his use of the general pause, or silence. This particular example, which begins the development section, although only a couple of seconds long, seems to last an eternity. It leads right back to the hurdy-gurdy tune in a startlingly different key. The music of the opening interrupts violently, only to be mocked with obvious glee by that cheap melody, its "oompah" rhythm reinforced by the woodwinds, but this too runs out of steam. Once again the hostility erupts (at 3:25), initiating a vigorous argument that stops suddenly with a few sharp chords. The hurdy-gurdy tune then sails in and shockingly breaks off, just like at the end of the exposition (at 3:58), only to start up once again in yet another strange key, its humor beginning to sound hollow thanks to a hesitant extension of its final phrase.

The opening music interrupts with renewed vigor, and just before it too runs completely out of gas, the major-key half of the exposition abruptly returns. The recapitulation thus begins (at 4:39) in midstream, as if nothing at all had happened, and with newfound confidence the music charges to the finish line—only to be mocked one last time by that insolent tune, which has the last word. It's a very disturbing movement, and one that certainly annoyed some contemporary critics who castigated Haydn for his lack of seriousness. The music takes the listener on an emotional roller-coaster ride of a kind absolutely unique to this composer: you won't hear anything even remotely like it in Mozart or Beethoven, and as mentioned before, it isn't until Mahler that this particular kind of subversive humor makes its way back into the symphonic tradition.

Symphony No. 45 in F-sharp Minor ("Farewell") (1772)

First Movement (CD 1, Track 7)
Scoring: 2 oboes, bassoon, 2 horns, and strings

Here you find the style that Symphony No. 80 mocks, and there's no denying that making fun of it took a huge amount of guts. Everything about this symphony is remarkable, even extraordinary. It is the only symphony in the key of F-sharp minor in the entire eighteenth century (and probably the nine-teenth as well). So unusual was this key that Haydn had to have special parts made for the horns so that they could play the music at all. Its first movement, if both repeats are observed, contains more than eight minutes of the most relentless violence ever conceived. Only about sixty seconds' worth of music in total could by any stretch of the imagination be considered a melody, and its sole purpose is to make the surrounding maelstrom sound even more vicious in contrast. Certainly no earlier music comes anywhere close in sheer intensity, and it would be well into the romantic period before anyone would even try.

Despite this, and the fact that the finale's closing measures leave an impression of wistful sadness, the symphony ends with a joke, an actual early example of "performance art." As the tale goes, the members of Haydn's band, trapped with their employer in his Hungarian swamp of a palace at Eszterháza—with their wives and children forced to remain in far-off Vienna—begged their Kapellmeister to do something about their lamentable situation. So Haydn conceived a finale that, beginning like a typical fast conclusion, breaks off and starts anew with an adagio in which players each have a little solo, blow out their candle, take their music and their instrument, and leave, until at last only two solo violins (Haydn and his concertmaster) bring the work to its lonely conclusion. According to legend, Prince Nicholas got the message immediately and ordered everyone back to Vienna the next day. There is no reason to doubt the truth of this story, but it hardly explains the music's alteration between almost hysteri-cal anger and despair on the one hand and benumbed calm on the other.

Or does it? You have already seen how the sonata principle

adapts itself to the musical content in question. Given the fact that the symphony must have been written around Haydn's concept for its ending, his challenge then becomes finding a way to make everything that comes before point to the finale as a necessary resolution, however remarkable it may be. Exactly how he does this in terms of the work as a whole I leave you to investigate at your leisure, but it stands to reason that the main job of the first movement will be to define the terms of the task ahead, and it further seems logical that the extremely unconventional conclusion requires an equally startling or unusual opening, which is exactly what Haydn provides.

As in Symphony No. 80's first-movement exposition, there's no point in worrying about such technical terms as "first subject" and "second subject" here. Indeed, from a purely melodic point of view there is no second subject at all, but you wouldn't call this movement monothematic so much as "monotextural." The entire exposition comes across as a single unified entity, bound together by

- the lack of symmetrical melody—almost all the motives (one hesitates to call them tunes) are in fact nothing more than arpeggios, or broken chords, which do little more than outline the harmony of the space that they occupy;
- the syncopated rhythm in the second violins that persists almost throughout the entire movement;
- the wailing oboes in long notes atop the more feverishly churning strings.

All these elements articulate the contrast between major and minor tonalities, and between loud and soft. Notice also that as with Symphony No. 80's first movement, the music is written in 3/4 (you may not catch the actual time signature, but the feel of being "in three" is unmistakable). It may seem surprising that

Haydn writes some of his harshest music in what is effectively a dance rhythm. Indeed, nearly half of his symphonies open with movements in triple time (as opposed to about 25 percent for Mozart), but this meter gives the music tremendous energy and "swing," which is why it's associated with the dance in the first place.

The exposition comes to a close at 2:47. At first it seems as if the development will consist of exactly the same kind of music, although it starts in a more hopeful major key. But this pulls up short with three abrupt chords, and at 3:29, a totally new, lyrical melody begins. This tune is remarkable in many respects. In the first place, it really is a tune, the only one in the movement. Although subtly related to what has come before (you can hear the three-chord formula clearly in its accompaniment), it feels completely alien in its surroundings. It also sounds much slower in tempo owing to the shape of its phrases, but in reality, the speed hasn't changed at all. It's still moving forward at the same anxious pace. The melody fails to establish anything resembling a firm rhythm or shape: it wanders distractedly from one phrase to the next, rootless (literally—there's very little bass underpinning), and then it breaks off as suddenly as it started, as if in midsentence.

Suddenly the music of the opening comes blasting back in (at 4:16), but instead of a regular recapitulation, Haydn goes right on developing the material, rearranging its various components to achieve the maximum emotional intensity right up to the movement's final bar. If the result in Symphony No. 80 was disturbing but funny, then this is just plain upsetting, even tragic. The emotional and formal extremes to which Haydn pushes the music turn out to have a single purpose: to provide a beginning so expressively lopsided that only a very special finale will be able to bring the piece to a satisfying conclusion.

String Quartet in D Major, Op. 64, No. 5 ("Lark") (1790)

First Movement (CD 2, Track 2)

This is one of Haydn's most popular quartets, not just because of the "lark" tune in the opening movement but also on account of its brilliant finale. If its first movement were a movie, it would be *The Attack of the Killer Triplets*. The tempo is a placid allegro moderato, and in this musical equivalent of suburban comfort the piece clearly wishes to remain. The initial subject contains two themes, the first of which is a staccato folk song on second violin, viola, and cello. This is immediately repeated, but as an accompaniment to the lark melody on the first violin (a flexibility very typical of Haydn's quartet writing in general).

Some lyrical motion music (at 0:31) leads to a very different second subject (at 0:54). It contains no true tunes at all—remember, the first subject featured two for the price of one—but consists instead of syncopated chords outlining spicy, dissonant harmonies. You may recall that the first movement of the "Farewell" Symphony used very similar syncopations and dissonances, but here, at this relaxed tempo, they don't bite. They just provide rhythmic and harmonic contrast in comparison to the first subject. Tonal stability returns in the form of a cadence theme (at 1:19) that contains two runs of descending triplets. *Triplets* are simply three notes squeezed into the space of two, which means that they break up the basic rhythm even further and (in this case) also move more quickly than any other note values that Haydn has used thus far.

After the repeat, the development begins just like the exposition, with the lark tune in a new key. Those mischievous triplets break in (at 3:31) and knock the music off course. The lark attempts to sing again (at 3:50) but gets whacked out of its nest by an aggravated second subject, whose dissonances now sound pained. Suddenly, a storm of triplets takes over the entire quartet (at 4:10), and as it dissipates, the opening theme returns to begin the recapitulation—except the triplets don't know it's the reca- pitulation, and they cavort around both the motion music and the second subject, which is barely recognizable (at 5:06), caus- ing the music to break off in frustration. And so Haydn begins the recapitulation all over again, this time starting immediately with the lark melody underpinned by a smooth, steady rhythm in eighth notes from the second violin and viola.

This musical "fence" succeeds in keeping the triplets at bay. As an extra precaution, Haydn omits the original motion music entirely and skips straight to the second subject, whose disso- nances have largely evaporated even though the rhythm remains the same, while the triplets in the cadence theme behave them- selves perfectly, bringing the music to a quiet close, with order restored.

As you can clearly hear, the story that this movement tells is entirely different from that of the two symphonic movements just discussed, as is the thematic material and the movement's form. Indeed, the only thing the six opening movements in sonata form heard so far have in common is the fact that each one's unique shape is governed by its own special themes and motives—a unity founded on diversity, if you will.

I want to close this discussion by returning to a subject raised initially in chapter 1: Haydn's use of vocal-style melodies. As you can plainly hear, all these movements have recourse to what you might call "song," but this is only one melodic type among many. You have also heard themes in broken chords, ideas consisting of simple rhythmic gestures, blocks of harmony without any tune at all, subjects consisting of motives presented both simultaneously and in dialogue, and melodies that, however memorable, are too asymmetrical or unstable in shape to be easily sung. The emo- tional range of this material runs the gamut from intense anguish to pastoral joy, lyrical sophistication to lowbrow comedy, and melodramatic exaggeration to folklike innocence. These varied musical ideas and the formal shapes that they generate have one purpose only: to support an equally wide expressive vocabulary. It therefore follows that the best way to understand the music is not to worry about "form" but to listen without preconceptions to the particular way in which each movement delivers its specific message.

6
Slow Movements

At one time I asked Haydn jokingly if it was true that he composed the andante with the timpani stroke [Symphony No. 94 ("Surprise")] to wake up any of the English who might have fallen asleep during the concert. "No," he replied, "but I was motivated to surprise the public with a novelty, so that my student Pleyel, who at that time (1792) had been hired by a London orchestra, and whose concerts started a week prior to mine, would not upstage me. The opening allegro of my symphony received countless bravos, but the excitement of the audience reached its highpoint during the andante with the timpani stroke. Encore! Encore! resounded from each throat, and even Pleyel congratulated me on my idea.

—G. A. Griesinger

Haydn had to be the first composer in history whose slow movements were as famous as—and if anything, even bigger attractions than—his quick ones. A good number of Haydn symphonies with nicknames take them from their slow movements, and there's another, equally interesting fact related to the symphonies. Approximately forty of them have slow movements designated "adagio" or something similarly measured (lento, largo, grave); whereas out of fifty-one or so Mozart symphonies, only a single work (the "Linz" Symphony, No. 36) contains an adagio, and it's a "poco adagio" at that (*poco* means "a little bit" or "slightly"). Haydn's cultivation of the symphonic adagio, therefore, is an important stylistic fingerprint, and it stems directly from his willingness to use musical materials of a nonvocal character or, as you will also hear, his ability to use singable ideas in unusual ways.

The reason that you will seldom find an adagio in a Mozart symphony stems from the fact that any instrumental piece in slow tempo based on song-type tunes needs to move at a "human" pace (basically andante, or walking tempo) in order to preserve its vocal identity. The phrases have to breathe the way a singer would, particularly if the players are wind instruments, which operate on the same principle as the human voice and so need to pause regularly for breath. On the other hand, although Haydn wrote plenty of such "singing" andantes (the other 60-odd percent of his symphonies, in fact), his very slow movements—whether in sonata, variation, rondo, or some other form entirely—often feature a combination of hymnlike melodies of a religious nature, strange or evocative harmonies, and arresting sonorities found nowhere else among his works. In short, Haydn has a special "adagio style," and through it he introduced instrumental music to an entirely new emotional world—that of the spiritual, or transcendental, becoming the first composer to reach beyond the standard happy/sad antithesis typical of most compositions without voices.

Haydn's spirituality has been one of the least discussed and acknowledged aspects of both his character and his art. Everyone concedes that he was deeply religious but then usually goes on to say that he was "cheerful" and that his faith did not compromise his natural exuberance or high spirits. And why should it? Where is it written that all those with strong spiritual leanings have to be miserable, or austere, or inhibited? Aside from this obvious point, both scholars and commentators are not only uncomfortable discussing religion in general, often for purely personal reasons, they also have problems studying spiritual components in music within the commonly accepted vocabulary of theory and analysis. It's all very subjective, they will tell you, and therefore beyond the sphere of legitimate subjects for consideration. Humor in music, for example, can be reduced to matters of timing, rhythm, dynamic contrasts, and harmonic surprise. There's no guarantee a listener will get the joke, but at least it's explicable. Transcendental qualities, on the other hand, would seem to offer nearly insuperable difficulties to the prospective analyst, despite the fact that most people today are probably far more open to the notion that music without words can express these feelings than they are to the possibility of its being truly funny.

And yet, Haydn himself stressed the "moral" character of his instrumental music. He began all his major works with the words "In Nomine Domini" (In the name of the Lord) and concluded them with "Laus Deo" (Praise God), written directly into the score. He was the foremost composer of liturgical music of his age (although he would have accorded that honor to his brother Michael, who wound up with what would have been Mozart's job in Salzburg). Of course, it's one thing to describe religious music that purports to support a specific text and that belongs to a longstanding tradition, such as that of the Catholic church, and it's quite another matter to attempt to quantify the vaguer, more generalized spiritual or sublime element in an abstract chamber or orchestral composition. Still, there's no question that many of Haydn's works in these genres express exactly this quality.

Two examples illustrate this very special type of instrumental writing, which not only enriched Haydn's and Beethoven's art but also had an inestimable impact on much later music, from Wagner (who was a big admirer of Haydn) to Bruckner, Mahler, the so-called Second Viennese School (Schoenberg, Berg, Webern), and beyond. The first extract does not come from a symphony at all but from Haydn's oratorio *The Creation,* the opening of which is a tone poem (probably the first legitimate example of that genre as well), *The Representation of Chaos,* which illustrates the biblical text: "and the earth was without form, and void." In this prelude, Haydn achieves the paradox of creating music that portrays formlessness in a manner that is atmospheric, evocative, specific, and (believe it or not) formally satisfying. Here's how he does it:

The Creation (1798)

Largo: The Representation of Chaos *(CD 2, Track 14)*
Scoring: 2 flutes, 2 oboes, 2 clarinets, 2 bassoons,
　　　　　contrabassoon, 2 trumpets, 2 horns, 3 trombones,
　　　　　timpani, and strings

The first thing to keep in mind is that *chaos* does not mean "noise and hysteria" but "disorder." However, even before Haydn gets to that part, he needs his empty void, something music of all the arts is particularly well suited to express. The piece opens with a loud octave C in all the instruments, whose range from low to high suggests both depth and distance, while the total lack of harmonic filler admirably qualifies this sound as a void. The initial attack and decrescendo, combined with the very large and weighty orchestration, also conveys a sense of brooding power. At a stroke, Haydn has provided listeners with the musical equivalent of a big, vacant space, and everything that comes afterward clearly appears to move within and around it.

　　Common sense dictates that in order to maintain the impression of disorder, Haydn will not write any symmetrical tunes. Instead, he offers a series of short motives that drift about unpredictably but nevertheless have very specific emotional qualities. The soft sound of muted strings that arises out of the void is intensely lonely and sad. This inchoate musical matter longs for order, for harmony, and suffers in its absence. But it is an other-worldly, suprahuman sorrow. (Similarly, the moment when God brings forth light represents, as depicted by the massed voices of the chorus and the full orchestra, a greater-than-human joy.) Some of the objects adrift in Haydn's vacant musical cosmos include

- a seven-note rising figure in triplets, first on bassoon, then on viola (at 0:44);
- a heavy rhythm in the strings with sorrowful cries in oboes and flutes (at 2:21);
- a series of abrupt chords in the strings (at 2:53);
- a three-note dotted rhythm (dum, dadum) in oboes and horns over rippling clarinets, full of stabbing dissonance (at 3:00), punctuated by heavy orchestral thuds.

After these motives pass from view, an upward run on solo clarinet leads to the most remarkable passage yet, a genuine piece of "space music" featuring softly pulsating high violins and winds above low cellos and basses, with nothing at all in the middle. Haydn, incidentally, when in England visited the famous astronomer (and oboist, and composer) William Herschel, discoverer of the planet Uranus. The two men discussed music as well as astronomy. It was while Haydn was gazing out into space, according to legend, that the first ideas for *The Creation* came to him, and he was evidently familiar with the Nebular Hypothesis (first proposed in 1775), which held that the planets gradually condensed out of clouds of dust and gas. It's hard not to hear something similar to this idea in *Chaos*.

The space music gradually drifts toward a return to the movement's opening gesture (at 4:15), but instead of a single blast of emptiness, Haydn hammers out seven rapid cannon shots in the triplet rhythm of the initial rising bassoon figure. The void, in other words, is no longer empty. The concluding moments clearly recapitulate the opening pages as all the initial motives return in varied form, suggesting not just aimless wandering but an imperceptible evolution and coalescence. At last desolate strings and solo flute bring the music to a mournful close in utter darkness, but in an unambiguous minor-key harmony that's all the more powerful for being so soft and so stable. However hesitant and uncertain, the process of creation has begun, and all stands in readiness for the Divine Will to make itself manifest.

This astonishing piece of music, although admirably illustrative of its subject, in fact relies on quite a few stylistic fingerprints with which you are already familiar: the lack of literal repetition, the shortened recapitulation, unexpected harmonies and rhythms, asymmetrical phrases, soloistic scoring for wind instruments, and above all, an avoidance of anything like a singable tune. The very slow tempo sets all these traits into high relief, and this, combined with the fact that there are no obvious external references at all (to nature, for example) creates the music's "spacey" feel.

Symphony No. 86 in D Major (1786)

Capriccio: Largo (CD 1, Track 10)
Scoring: flute, 2 oboes, 2 bassoons, 2 horns, and strings

This is the third largo you have heard so far. It comes from the set of six "Paris" Symphonies (Nos. 82–87) that Haydn composed for the French capital, and like *Chaos* and the slow movement of Symphony No. 88, this largo seems to create its own form—big time. Indeed the very word *capriccio,* which means "capricious," stands very close to the idea of "chaos," and so does the music. While totally different in content, it shares many of the same principles of design and treatment, and even a few sonorities. On the other hand, Haydn comes right out and tells his listeners exactly what *Chaos* represents, while here he offers no verbal clues at all to the music's expressive message. Is it spiritual, sublime, or something else entirely? Listen, and judge for yourself.

Like *Chaos*, this movement places a series of musical "objects" in a contrasting and unpredictable relationship to each other. There are four:

1. The opening gesture of three rising notes (incidentally, one of the symphony's principal unifying elements) leading to a brief sort of chorale. Musically this acts like a doorway, or arch, usually repeated immediately but never resolving exactly the same way twice. Listen particularly to the haunting modulation at 3:09, which foreshadows the similarly magical moment between the two themes of the adagio in Beethoven's Ninth.

2. The arch leads to a song, but one that immediately begins to move in curious directions. One of the main ways that composers (Beethoven especially) evoke the transcendental and the sublime in slow tempos is not by ignoring songs but by writing extreme examples of them—that is, music of song-like character, but so slow, ornate, elaborate, sustained, and harmonically complex that it sounds more than merely human. This is a particularly fine example. In Beethoven you will find entire movements built on this single principle, but in Haydn, typically, it is merely one of several ideas, all jostling for your attention.

3. The song pauses now and then to listen to a gentle little fanfare motive (at 1:06) and then gives way to a sudden eruption of emotion (at 1:51) that exhausts itself almost as abruptly as it began.

4. Haydn concludes the movement's opening section with a series of loud chords separated by pauses (at 2:19), very similar to those at 2:53 in *Chaos*.

Also close to that later work is the haunting passage of cool, desolate space music at 3:13, with its pulsing strings, solo flute on

high, and groping cellos and basses below. Like the corresponding moment in *Chaos,* this episode leads to its exact opposite, the
angriest and most passionate version of no. 3. Pay special attention to Haydn's use of silence in this piece. At quick tempos—for
example, the opening of Symphony No. 80—a pause can be
very funny or add an element of surprise. Here, on the other
hand, silence only increases the overall feeling of timelessness
and mystery.

As for the remainder of the movement, listen to how Haydn
varies and organizes these four elements, so sharply differentiated from each other that their distinctive shapes almost become
visual. When I concentrate on this music, I sometimes imagine
myself wandering back and forth through an outdoor sculpture
garden or ancient ruin, looking at the different objects in the
changing light over the course of an afternoon. You may also want
to check out the similarly amazing second-movement fantasia
from the String Quartet in E-flat Major, Op. 76, No. 6, a piece
of music so "spaced out" that for much of its length, Haydn writes
without any key signature at all.

One of the very greatest writers on Haydn, British musicolo-
gist Donald Francis Tovey, has noted that this movement is actually in a clear sonata form, and indeed it does roughly fall into
three sections that might well be described as an exposition with
first and second subjects, a development, and a recapitulation. On
the other hand, everything about the music conspires to create
an air of sublime mystery, largely by contradicting any rational
expectations as to its structure and treatment of tonality. You
might better call it a "sonata improvisation," for that is how it
sounds, but far more interesting than the question of form is the
fact that Tovey has (perhaps instinctively) recognized the music's
spiritual character in noting a similarity between this movement's
"song" passage and a section ("Passus et sepultus est") from the
Crucifixus of Beethoven's *Missa solemnis.*

String Quartet in G Major, Op. 33, No. 5 (1781)

Largo cantabile (CD 2, Track 3)

We now turn from the sublime to the ridiculous, qualities that have more in common musically than you might suspect. Specifically, expressing either feeling usually involves some form of exaggeration, and a very slow tempo is just one of these extreme characteristics. In this particular example, Haydn presents an aria for the first violin, which behaves very much like an operatic diva. The tone is tragic, deeply so, a characteristic intensified by the static accompaniment, the tempo, the regularity of the tune, and the increasing ornamentation of the melodic line, which varies considerably on its return. Formally this movement really is an *aria* (or song) in ABA form, the central B section turning to a brighter tonality.

The first A section ends with a sort of refrain at 0:43, and this returns (one would think) to round off the movement. But no— after this huge outpouring of melodramatic emotion, the quartet blows the whole thing away with a derisive pizzicato *plink*. The music is deliciously ambiguous: is the violin solo serious or not? Much depends on how much the player decides to ham it up, and also on that final *plink,* which Haydn marks at a healthy forte but which many quartets refuse to accept at face value and tone down, attempting to maintain the serious mood to the end.

These Op. 33 quartets, which Haydn claimed were composed "in a totally new and special way," caused a sensation throughout Europe. They provided the models for Mozart's equally epochal set of six quartets dedicated to his best friend, which in turn led to Haydn's famous statement to Mozart's father about his son being "the best composer known to me either in person or by reputation." They are most famous, though, for replacing their minuet movements with a *scherzo* (joke), representing Haydn's first systematic attempt to make comedy an integral part of his musical idiom and of the classical style in general. They are, in fact, often hilarious, and as this example shows, not just in their scherzos.

Piano Trio No. 44 (28) in E Major (1797)

Allegretto (CD 2, Track 9)

This is the first of three very different variation movements offered for your consideration, and one of Haydn's most affecting. Its basic form is that of a passacaglia, or a series of free variations over a repeated bass line, only in this case, Haydn varies the bass line as well: not a lot, but enough to provide additional textural variety and make the changes in harmony from minor to major— and back again—more powerful. Like many of Haydn's pieces in variation form, although this is technically a "slow movement," its actual tempo isn't that slow at all. The music begins with all three instruments (piano, violin, and cello) in unison announcing the bass theme. Once this is over, the strings drop out, and the piano offers the principal melody.

Very baroque in style, this tune has a certain relentless sadness that's quite arresting—I say relentless because of the "walking" bass below that keeps up its steady procession of notes in even rhythm. After one full turn through the tune in the minor, Haydn shifts to the major for a repetition (at 0:35) that broadens out into an independent episode. Note just how far apart the pianist's hands are at 0:57. There's something oddly disturbing about music that's all top and bottom with nothing in the middle, as you may have noticed in considering *Chaos* and the capriccio of Symphony No. 86. It has a certain element of danger, heightened in this case by the more rapid tempo and the bare, two-part writing. It's all the more stunning, then, when Haydn finally permits the pianist some consoling harmony (at 1:15), and this signals the return of the violin and cello (at 1:25), whose softening influence turns the melody almost into a lullaby.

From this plateau of peace, Haydn very gradually shades the music in darker tones, until the minor-key version of the tune returns, violently this time, only now the tune has become the bass, and what was the bass is now the melody, passionately sung by the violin. The eruption subsides after one full statement of the tune, the music rights itself, and the mood returns to that of the movement's beginning. But no: the melody stops in midphrase, and after three questioning flourishes on the piano, Haydn slams the door closed with two loud, stern minor chords.

Aside from packing such a powerful emotional punch, looking back, you might describe the overall form of this movement as a combination variation, ABA (that is: minor–major–minor) and passacaglia all in one, and its intensity, as usual with Haydn, arises directly from the organic manner in which the form evolves from the musical materials themselves. The principal melody belongs to the song type, but the unusual treatment gives it a particularly impressive expressive force, and coaxes it into revealing several contrasting moods over the course of a movement lasting scarcely three minutes. It's a telling example of the fact that in Haydn, thematic economy never compromises emotional intensity.

Symphony No. 94 ("Surprise") (1792)

Andante (CD 1, Track 8)
Scoring: 2 flutes, 2 oboes, 2 bassoons, 2 horns, 2 trumpets,
timpani, and strings

This is "feel good" music, a piece so delightful—so full of charm, grace, warmth, and color—that it practically smiles at you and dares you not to smile back. It's also probably the most famous symphonic variation movement in existence. The tune is a fake folk song of the "Twinkle, Twinkle Little Star" variety (that melody, which is really a French nursery rhyme, has also been used by other composers as a subject for variations, including a famous piano solo by Mozart). Normal variations on a single theme usually break the subject in half, and each half gets repeated: AABB. Haydn places his famous surprise where you would least expect it, just before the first B. If the repeats themselves are varied, as often happens, then the variation is quite reasonably called a *double variation*.

Haydn's movement takes the following form:

Theme	The second half of A gets repeated extra softly, setting up the "surprise," while the second half of B adds lovely wind scoring to the basic string sonority. So the melody has already been varied before the variations actually begin, just as Haydn's sonata-allegro music often develops before reaching the formal development section.
Variation 1 0:59	A strict AABB shape, beginning with yet another loud surprise, which not incidentally "explains" the first one and so keeps it from sounding merely gratuitous. The tune is in the lower strings, with decorations touched in by the first violins.
Variation 2 1:56	In a stern minor key, the A section is repeated literally, but B gets so worked up that it breaks the bounds of the form entirely and is through-composed (contains no significant repetitions).
Variation 3 2:57	A solo oboe does its very best duck imitation, while the repeat of A substitutes delicate "toy music" on the upper winds and strings. The toy music continues into B and its identical repeat.

Variation 4	Bold horns and trumpets have the tune against
3:54	surging strings, but the repeat of A returns to
	the strings-only texture of variation 1. This same
	scoring dominates the first run through B, but
	the repeat is scored for horns and trumpets as
	was the first half of A.

Variation 5 (Coda)	Autumnal harmonies usher in a nostalgic
5:06	version of the theme on oboe and bassoon,
	while soft timpani and sustained strings bathe
	the music in a sunset glow. In this mood,
	woodwinds gently chirp the movement to
	a close.

Symphony No. 100 ("Military") (1794)

Allegretto (CD 1, Track 9)
Scoring: 2 flutes, 2 clarinets, 2 oboes, 2 bassoons, 2 horns,
2 trumpets, timpani, "Turkish" percussion (bass drum,
cymbals, triangle), and strings

Another not-very-slow movement that gave the entire symphony its nickname, this particular variation structure can be viewed in two different ways: as a simple ABA with a huge coda attached or as something close to Haydn's patented form based on alternating major and minor melodies. He wrote many movements of this type in strict style, with regular repeats and clearly marked variations of each tune, the most famous being the Andante with Variations in F Minor for solo piano and the slow movement in Symphony No. 103 ("Drumroll"). This particular example's formal freedom arises primarily from the spectacular use of the percussion (for the first time in any symphony that matters), which tends to carve up the piece into episodes with those special instruments versus those without. Amazingly, Haydn borrowed and adapted this music from his Lira Concerto No. 3 in G (see chapter 10 for details), where, as scored for small orchestra, he called it a "romance."

The music begins somewhat like its companion in the "Surprise" Symphony, in that the theme itself has varied repeats initially: A (strings and flutes), A (woodwinds and horns), B (strings and flutes), B (woodwinds and horns). Because the melody is quite a bit longer in its B section than the previous example, Haydn finds room only for a couple of variations. The second theme (or central section, if you consider the movement to be in song form) enters at 1:55, along with the percussion and the turn to a minor key. In keeping with his frequent practice, this new(ish) tune is based on the same motives as the preceding one. The theme's second half, which is repeated literally in threatening crescendo like an advancing army (at 2:24), is particularly impressive and powerful.

The opening tune returns with varied scoring, and the brilliant wind and percussion writing might lead one to overlook the divided violas throughout the movement that enrich the string section as well. Haydn extends and develops the major-key melody freely, with several percussion eruptions, and moves gradually to an expectant close. A fanfare at 5:08 for the second trumpet—Haydn likes to give everyone a moment to shine—in fact turns out to be the same Austrian military call that begins Mahler's Fifth Symphony over a hundred years later. It leads to a huge timpani crescendo as the orchestra explodes into the minor once again. A shuddering diminuendo leads to a timid variation of some of the second theme (or middle section) material, before the melodic turn common to both develops into a full coda. This, then, is a very concise movement overall, despite its huge sound and grandly processional character. In the soft episode just before the end (at 5:55), Haydn basks in the same autumnal harmonies heard at the conclusion of the andante in the "Surprise"

Symphony; then trumpets, timpani, and percussion close the movement with a heroic flourish.

Like the pastoral scene (and possibly also the largo) in Symphony No. 88 and, of course, *The Representation of Chaos,* this movement is illustrative, or *program,* music. In Haydn's day, the romantic era's polarization between two schools of musical expression—descriptive music on the one hand (represented by Wagner and Liszt) and absolute or abstract music on the other (represented by Brahms)—had not yet settled into opposing camps engaged in a pitched cultural war. Haydn himself, ever the pragmatist, had no problem using music for descriptive purposes as long as the subject itself was in his view suitable for musical treatment—hence, his famous remark in connection with the libretto of his oratorio *The Seasons:* "I have been an industrious man all my life, but it would never have occurred to me to set industry to music!"

For Haydn's audience, the use of Turkish percussion inevitably evoked the actual sounds of battle. Trumpets and timpani were, in fact, true military instruments at that time. When a composer needed timpani, he requisitioned them from the local armory, and they were used as often on horseback on the field of battle as in the concert hall. However, the rollicking finale of this symphony, in a typical Haydn transformation, both reintroduces and in the process demilitarizes the percussion, so as to have its brilliance on hand for the symphony's rousing climax. Not only does this strategy help unify the work by the simple use of timbre alone, it shows that even lowly, noise-making instruments are capable of emotional shadings.

When this enlarged percussion section once again returns to the symphony orchestra in the finale of Beethoven's Ninth some three decades later (after a brief stopover in Friedrich Witt's colorful "Turkish" Symphony of 1809), you will hear it put to exactly the same dual use, first in its utilitarian role as

the rhythm section of a military march and then supporting
the closing chorus in praise of joy. It would be nearly a century
before another symphonist, in the person of Gustav Mahler,
working outside of what had then become the German tradition,
rediscovered how to treat percussion (and many other new and
unusual sounds as well) in a manner that supported his music's
development and overall formal cohesion. But you can find the
very same technique at work in Haydn, not in some embryonic
or primitive form, but with a full understanding and use of its
limitless potential—even in his slow movements.

Minuets / Scherzos

I genuinely wish someone would try to write a really new minuet.

—Joseph Haydn

If Johann Strauss II was "the waltz king," then Haydn was unquestionably "the minuet king." No one comes anywhere close to him with respect to the innovative qualities that he packed into this simple dance form in three-quarter time. His achievement is almost totally unappreciated today, if only because few understand just how many perfunctory, excruciatingly dull minuets were written in Haydn's time. Trust me: it's a big number. Exactly how many Haydn himself wrote, both as movements in larger works as well as actual music for the ballroom, remains a mystery, but estimates hover in the vicinity of about a thousand. Even in his own lifetime, Haydn's minuets were celebrated for their combination of vitality, toe-tapping rhythms, sophisticated craftsmanship, and unforgettable tunes. Because the minuet offers very little scope for formal innovation, I have selected just three for discussion here, but all of them are "really new" in the best sense of the term.

As noted in considering Symphony No. 88 in chapter 2, minuets designed for use in symphonic or instrumental contexts are not so much dances in a literal sense as they are stylizations of the dance concept: in other words, their most prominent musical characteristic is rhythm. In addition, the second half of the main section often begins with a miniature, sonata-style development before returning to the opening of the minuet proper. The combination of strong rhythmic impetus with the opportunity to vary themes and motives in accordance with the sonata principle plays to Haydn's basic strengths, and so despite the relatively fixed formal pattern, you will find as much melodic variety in his minuets as in any other movement type that he used.

One of the most basic things to listen for in any minuet is the contrast between the outer sections and the central trio (which, as mentioned previously, just means "middle section"). Haydn saves some of his most startling inspirations for these small, independent episodes. They can include anything, from merely an alternate kind of dance (very frequent), to a miniconcerto (Symphony No. 51), pastoral tone painting (Symphony No. 88), exotic excursions into Hungarian or Gypsy music (Symphony No. 60 ["Il distratto"]), and even surprising eruptions of tragic emotion (String Quartet in C Major, Op. 54, No. 2). There are no rules governing what goes into a trio, so it's impossible to predict what you are most likely to hear.

Haydn also shows great flexibility in where he puts his minuets. They can usually be found among the middle movements of a four-movement work, the standard placement being in the third position, but the real determining factor is always where the music most requires the rhythmic kick that a dance piece provides. In the piano sonatas and trios, which Haydn often treats as lighter in style than the contemporaneous symphonies and string quartets, the minuet (or some other type of dance movement) often does duty as the finale, particularly when it comes to works having only two or three movements. A few relatively early symphonies also have minuet finales: Nos. 4, 9, 18, 26, and 30, and they too feature just three movements. Since there are no string quartets having less than four movements, none of them place the minuet last.

Symphony No. 77 in B-flat Major (1782)

Menuetto: Allegro (CD 1, Track 11)
Scoring: flute, 2 oboes, 2 bassoons, 2 horns, and strings

There are three major points worth mentioning in connection with this delightful movement. The first concerns the tempo: many listeners expect something slowish and pompous in connection with the word *minuet*, probably because the ones in Mozart's last symphonies (as well as in Beethoven's Eighth) employ a moderate tempo and tend to emphasize the dance's more courtly aspect. Haydn wrote quite a few in a similar vein, like the one in the "Military" Symphony, for instance. But often he marks the tempo, as here, at a genuine allegro, giving the music additional lightness or a vigorously rhythmic, very nonaristocratic, spring to its step. Actually, many Haydn minuets sound much closer to folk music or that precursor of the waltz, the *ländler*. Too many performers of the traditional school (not the period instrument folks) still take these movements much too slowly, as if *minuet* means "allegretto" and no faster, with deathly dull results.

This movement, then, is a quick minuet, but the second major point you will notice is that this piece isn't waltzlike or particularly folksy at all. Just the opposite: it is a very witty and sophisticated study in syncopated rhythm (that is, the accents never fall on regular beats, which in a minuet means the first quarter note of each measure). To see what I mean, just try counting "*One,* two, three, *One,* two, three," while the music is actually playing. The rhythm gets so confused in the minuet's second half (at 0:16) that the music comes to a complete halt in order to gather itself for the return of the opening section. Haydn loved syncopations and rhythmic games; he was probably the biggest fan of off-beat accents before Stravinsky, and many of his minuets deliberately upset the regular stresses typical of true dance music. The suggestion of ballroom guests tripping over themselves is often quite funny, highlighted here by the absolutely even rhythm of the accompaniment below the wildly asymmetrical melody.

The tune in both halves of the trio (at 0:58) is clearly based on the two corresponding parts of the minuet, but now the rhythm is regular, with all the musical wrinkles ironed out. The contrast is more than just charming: it makes the trio sound like a sort of primitive country cousin of the ultrachic but oddly eccentric minuet. Perhaps one day, when this tune grows up, it will learn how to syncopate like its more urbane relative. Despite the fact that this movement lasts little more than two and half minutes, Haydn wrote it with the same craftsmanship and polish as his most expansive adagios or sonata allegros. Indeed, because the music is so concise and the form so simple, it gives the impression that Haydn has taken extra care to ensure that not a single note goes to waste or fails to make an impression.

String Quartet in G Major, Op. 76, No. 1 (1797)

Menuetto: Presto (CD 2, Track 5)

As mentioned previously, in his six Op. 33 string quartets, Haydn replaced the minuets with a scherzo, or "joke." However, aside from a superabundance of humor, these movements are still traditional minuets of either the allegretto or allegro type— although if you look at the proportion of quick minuets (four) to slow (two), the handwriting is clearly on the wall. Haydn began speeding up his minuets pretty regularly in his perpetual quest for something truly new and different. As early as the mid-1760s, he had used the scherzo designation, quite unusually, for the opening movement of his String Trio No. 6 in E-flat, but it was not until the 1790s that Haydn (along with Beethoven) hit on the true scherzo, a movement so swift that the three beats in each measure merge into one. Unlike his younger colleague, Haydn continued calling these pieces minuets, but their new character is unmistakable. What marks this music is not the particularized rhythm of a specific dance but simply the overwhelming impression of swift, inexorable movement heightened by unpredictable dynamics (such as the outburst that closes each section of this particular example, first heard at 0:05).

Although Haydn does not indicate a change of tempo for the trio (at 0:50), it's always played much slower than the minuet, partly owing to tradition and, more significantly, because the music demands it and no self-respecting player could possibly miss the point. This trio consists of a café or street-music solo for the first violin, accompanied by all the other players *pizzicato* (plucked), in regular rhythm. Just how much schmaltz the player brings to the party, and how convincingly he or she puts it across, is one of those things that separates the men from the boys, interpretively speaking. As in the previous example, the contrast between minuet and trio is extreme—even more so here, since the music of this middle section is unrelated to that of the presto, as is its texture and style. In fact, you can clearly hear that it is quite possible within an ensemble theoretically homogeneous in timbre (like a string quartet) to color the music almost as boldly as with the full orchestra.

Piano Trio No. 40 (26) in F-sharp Minor (1795)

Tempo di Menuetto (CD 2, Track 11)

This minuet is a finale—a tragic finale. Very few composers have understood and exploited the expressive possibilities of sorrowful dance music. Haydn was the first, although many commentators mistakenly credit Beethoven and the creepy scherzo of his Fifth Symphony with this innovation. Mahler was a sad/scary dance music specialist. Both Chopin and Dvořák had their moments too, while the twentieth century featured examples by composers as diverse as Ravel, Shostakovich, and Bartók. In a sense, Haydn's discovery isn't all that surprising, bearing in mind his desire to try everything, as well as his familiarity (like Mahler, Dvořák, Shostakovich, and others) with so much Hungarian and Slavic folk music employing exotic harmonies and minor keys. But the genius comes not in doing something first but in understanding what it means and so doing it best. Here you have one of the most successful of all such pieces, although it wasn't Haydn's first: consider the similarly sorrowful and impressively grim minuet finale of Symphony No. 26 ("Lamentazione").

What does it mean to write a tragic minuet? In order to answer this question optimally, you would have to listen to the entire piano trio and hear this finale in context. Its first movement is a mixture of happy and sad, but it comes across primarily as pensive and troubled. The adagio is so unforgettably beautiful that Haydn used it twice, in this work and in Symphony No. 102 (where it features some particularly fabulous orchestration— muted trumpets and timpani for the first time in a symphony). There's a big scholarly controversy over which version came first, symphony or trio, as if that matters. The point in this case is that the adagio, which flows along in a largely serene F-sharp major, represents an oasis of spiritual peace, an ideal state. Nothing signals a return to harsh reality better than a simple dance, and therein lies much of this movement's expressive power.

This minuet, then, evokes (for me anyway) the mundane dance of life, the need to go on, to maintain appearances, despite the crushing burden of grief that the music tries to suppress. However fanciful this interpretation may sound, the audible evidence supports it. For example, the first half of the main theme moves from melancholy minor to hopeful major, but its second half does just the opposite, and Haydn extends it past the return of the first part to ensure a dark and gloomy ending (at 1:09). This A section follows the traditional pattern of two halves, both repeated. The trio, which begins at 2:13, does not. Its first half, with repeat, features the violin in the most hopeful melody yet heard. It is, however, clearly a variation of the minuet, so this positive element has no independent existence. The second half (at 2:47) is through-composed. It turns right back into a dark minor key, graphically proving that brief ray of sunshine to be an illusion.

The minuet returns once again, played straight through. This time the second part runs directly into an extensive coda (at 4:37), which begins with a hauntingly ambivalent recollection of the trio, like the shadow of a memory, before a last reprise of bits of the minuet theme. Until this point, the emotional climate of the music has been rather subdued, the depth of sorrow suggested rather than made explicit. In the final bars, however, Haydn abandons any pretense of self-control and, with a shocking crescendo, a cry of despair concludes the work fortissimo.

Unlike this example, the majority of Haydn's minuets remain cheerful, upbeat crystallizations of the spirit of the dance. Very few multimovement works offer minuets the opportunity to shine that you can hear in this particular finale. What's most important to realize is the fact that Haydn clearly understood every musical possibility inherent in this outwardly stiff, less obviously expressive form. So whatever he chooses to do with it, you can rest assured that it will be the right thing in its place and that no opportunity has been overlooked simply because it's just "time for the usual minuet."

Finales
(Grand and Otherwise)

Haydn's theoretical rationale was very simple: specifically, a piece of music should have a fluent melody, coherent ideas, no unnecessary ornaments, nothing overworked, no excessively complicated accompaniments, etc. But how does one satisfy these requirements? That, he admitted, cannot be learned by studying the rules, but rather requires natural talent and the inspiration born of genius.

—G. A. Griesinger

There is no such thing as a specific finale form. The shape of the last movement often depends on what comes before, as well as on the interrelationships between a work's several parts. During your explorations of classical music in general, you will often hear mention of the so-called finale problem, which can be defined as the difficulty some composers theoretically experience in creating a satisfying ending to multimovement works. Most of the time, this comes up in discussions of large romantic symphonies, particularly ones that feel a necessity to follow the emotional curve of Beethoven's Fifth—a tragedy-to-triumph progression in which the finale supposedly resolves all the preceding angst and moodiness in a blaze of optimistic glory.

As a generalization concerning a valid issue in nineteenth-century aesthetics, this conception of the finale problem sometimes has its uses. As it relates to Haydn, however, the question more properly concerns the outwardly reasonable contention that it took him a lot of time, and much trial and error, before he invented just the right forms and sequence of movements suitable to a mature classical-period symphony or string quartet, with the finale being the most stubborn problem. This formulation relies on several mistaken assumptions:

1. The first of these places a qualitative value on differences between works largely on the basis of chronology. Did Haydn continue to evolve and grow as an artist right up to the end? Yes. Does this make his later finales inherently better than the earlier ones? Not necessarily. A 1790s era finale on a 1760s symphony would be just as unsatisfactory as the converse.

2. A second error arises out of the understandable desire to suggest that the finale problem has a single solution—that because first movements are almost always in sonata form, minuets in ABA, and so forth, composers need to find unique structures for finales as well (and that the musical universe is inherently a better place once they have). This flies in the face of perhaps the most basic tenet of the sonata principle, which is that forms, whether of individual movements or entire works, always shape themselves to the music's content, subject only to an overall tonal framework.

3. There is also a very commonly stated generalization that classical-period works begin with their most important movement and then relax formally and intellectually as the music progresses. Even when true, the fact that the most intellectually complex movement on paper in many sonata-style works will be the first one does not mean that it is the most significant, sophisticated, or expressive. Any number of additional, equally valid criteria may be cited in making this determination.

For example, you have already seen that several of Haydn's late works (the "Surprise" and "Military" Symphonies, for example) seem to have been built around their slow movements. His equally famous "Emperor" Quartet has two expressive peaks: the adagio variations on the "Emperor's Hymn" and the turbulent finale. The quartets Opp. 9 and 17 are similarly bifurcated, but their weight is distributed differently: large opening movements in moderate tempo lead to simpler minuets, and then expansive adagios precede vivacious finales. Symphony No. 88, discussed in chapter 2, has a singularly light opening and an even lighter finale. Its weightiest movements are the central largo and minuet, despite their less intricate form, and this fact only adds to the music's overriding pastoral impression of folklike charm and simplicity. Symphony No. 98 is a "grand-finale symphony," and don't forget that many of Haydn's chamber works from all periods begin with variations or slow movements and not with a sonata allegro at all.

So the finale problem really is a misnomer, or at best a generalization of very limited value in considering Haydn's approach to finding the right conclusion for any given work. As with so much else in attempting to define a composer who almost never repeats himself, the issue must be examined on a case-by-case basis. If you take the time to do that, you will discover that Haydn's powers of invention and freedom from routine are nowhere more evident than in his finales from all periods. After hearing the following broad selection, I have no doubt that you will come to regard the arrival of the last movement as he obviously did: not as a problem but as an opportunity.

Best of all, and speaking from a purely practical point of view, because many of these finales are quite short, I can offer you an even dozen (aside from the two already discussed in previous chapters), representing almost every formal type and genre mentioned thus far—and then some—covering virtually the whole of Haydn's creative life. There's no better way to summarize and conclude this discussion of his instrumental works than with this final proof, not of a slow climb from artistic squalor to ultimate perfection, but of the fact that the most outstanding quality of his early works is their confidence and maturity, while that of his later works is their ongoing originality and youthfulness.

Finales in Sonata Form

Symphony No. 8 in G Major ("Le Soir") (1761)

"La Tempesta": Presto (CD 1, Track 14)
Scoring: flute, 2 oboes, bassoon, 2 horns, and strings

Haydn's first Esterházy employer, Prince Paul, was a big fan of Vivaldi. In order to show off his compositional credentials on being hired, as well as the talents of his top-notch orchestra, it has been plausibly suggested that Haydn conceived his "Morning, Noon, and Night" trilogy of symphonies (Nos. 6–8) in the tradition of the Italian master's *The Four Seasons*. This accounts not just for the music's descriptive aspects but also for the fact that each of these works belongs to a category of pieces known as the *sinfonia concertante,* or symphony with concerto elements mixed in. All the principal wind and string players, even the double bass, have important solos in one or several movements.

The finale of Symphony No. 8, then, combines program music with concerto elements, solo flute and violin particularly, all presented in compact sonata form. This multifaceted approach gives so much of Haydn's early music its greater substance when compared with that of his colleagues. Descriptive symphonies were not, for example, all that unusual. Haydn's friend and colleague (and imitator) Dittersdorf wrote scads of them. What makes Haydn's efforts special at all the stages of his career is the way he integrates these various formal and expressive ideas into a satisfying whole. The music operates at several different levels simultaneously and works successfully from whatever angle you choose to consider it.

As far as storms go, this one isn't especially terrifying— picturesque and a touch cartoonish rather, very much like Vivaldi's own examples. The flute (at 0:13 and afterwards) represents lightning, exactly as it would many decades later in the great storm chorus in the oratorio *The Seasons*. The violins graphically mimic gusts of wind and rain, while the development section (at 1:57) focuses once again on the flute's lightning bolts. Haydn even finds room for a vivacious cello solo (at 3:07) just before the end. This trilogy of symphonies remains among the most popular of Haydn's early works, particularly since they are as rewarding to play as they are to hear and perfect for chamber orchestras looking to strut their stuff.

Symphony No. 13 in D Major (1763)

Finale: Allegro molto (CD 1, Track 13)
Scoring: flute, 2 oboes, bassoon, 4 horns, timpani, and strings

Here is an exuberant finale that not only takes advantage of simultaneous combinations of melodies (counterpoint), but its four-note main motive later became famous in the finale of Mozart's "Jupiter" Symphony. This does not mean that Mozart borrowed from Haydn. In fact, both were simply making use of a very old, very common bit of musical fabric and treating it in their own distinctive way. This is why it's so important, in

Haydn and Mozart both, to understand the difference between originality of material and originality of treatment. No matter how great a composer is as a creator of tunes, in the final analysis, what matters even more is how those tunes are presented and developed.

The comparatively large contingent of horns and winds for a Haydn symphony of this period means that he has the opportunity to make the music unusually colorful, with the four-note motive serving both as a theme by itself and an accompaniment to other material (at 0:11, for example). The coda begins with this motive becoming the basis of a multipart pileup (at 2:43), just as happens in Mozart's symphony, and while the latter is certainly grander in scale and more ambitious in content, this modest forerunner has an infectious vitality all its own. Its monothematic sonata structure and contrapuntal textures create spaciousness based on the music's vertical density (i.e., its multiple layers of sound), even though its actual duration is relatively brief.

There's one more very interesting fact worth pointing out in connection with Haydn's early symphonies in general. Most of them employ some brand of sonata form more frequently than any other type of construction, in both first movements and finales, but also quite often in slow movements as well. Paradoxically, the more adept Haydn became at manipulating the sonata style generally, the less he relied on standardized versions of the actual form. Instead, he increasingly began to diversify the movement structures of his instrumental works to include variations, rondos, and numerous unique solutions of his own invention. In this respect, he differs strikingly from Mozart, whose love of symmetry resulted in an unwavering attachment to (and continuous enlargement of) what eventually became the textbook version of sonata form.

Piano Sonata No. 33 (20) in C Minor (1771)

Finale: Allegro (CD 2, Track 12)

This movement is the finale to what many consider to be the first great classical piano sonata. It precedes all of Mozart's and Beethoven's important works in the genre by decades and also forms one of the high points of Haydn's "Sturm und Drang" (Storm and Stress) period—see chapter 11 for further details on this score. You have already heard, in the discussion of minuets, how Haydn succeeded in realizing the tragic qualities inherent in dance music in minor keys. This movement is another example, for although it is technically in sonata form, its principal subject is clearly a quick minuet in the obligatory 3/4 time, one interrupted by turbulent, developmental episodes (such as the passage at 2:35). The additional dramatic energy of sonata form makes this finale more active and consequently less despairing than the simpler ABA form of the minuet finale to the Piano Trio in F-sharp Minor, with the result that you may well hear anger as well as sadness in this music.

Symphony No. 44 in E Minor ("Mourning") (1772)

Presto (CD 1, Track 15)
Scoring: 2 oboes, [bassoon,] 2 horns, and strings

Anger is the predominant characteristic of this marvelous, clenched fist of a finale from another of Haydn's great "Storm and Stress" works. If you recall the opening movement of the "Farewell" Symphony (No. 45) from chapter 4, then you will find the emotional ambiance of this music very familiar. Formally speaking, all you need to know to understand this movement completely is how to count to seven. This is the number of notes in the jagged motive that makes up the principal theme, and Haydn treats it with every bit as much obsessive intensity as you find in the first movement of Beethoven's Fifth. Note in particular the major-key oasis at 0:49, consisting entirely of this self-same motive, which illustrates very graphically just how much expressive variety Haydn obtains from even the simplest of materials. It's the kind of thing he did better than anyone.

The nickname "Mourning" (in German: *Trauersymphonie*), by the way, comes from the consoling adagio, which legend says Haydn wished played at his funeral. So here you have yet another symphony named for its slow movement, although when the sad occasion finally arrived, they played Mozart's Requiem.

String Quartet in C Major, Op. 74, No. 1 (1793)
Finale: Vivace (CD 2, Track 6)

This spectacularly fun finale is monothematic to the extent that just about everything in it derives from the first six notes of its opening tune, which also appears in several highly contrasted variants and so gives the impression of unusually rich and varied melodic content. The movement initially presents the main theme in a lyrical, songful version. Haydn immediately develops this into a *staccato* (detached) variation (at 0:10). Some motion music leads to a brilliant scurrying passage for the first violin with the main theme's first few notes as accompaniment (at 0:43). These same notes serve as the basis for the syncopated second subject (at 1:03), while the entire tune returns in a folk-dance variation that closes the exposition over a bagpipe bass (at 1:15).

The short development section (beginning at 2:56) uses the scurrying passage to reach a distant minor key (at 3:19), introducing a wonderful, pensive transformation of the second subject, which somehow miraculously morphs back into a completely recomposed recapitulation without revealing how it managed to get there. Haydn omits the staccato version of the main theme and builds the second subject to a generously lyrical climax. At 4:53, a spectacular coda begins in which Haydn explains the entire substance of the movement, one step at a time: it starts with the opening six notes of the first subject, turns them into the main melody's staccato variation, and then cuts directly to the folk-dance cadence theme with some second-subject syncopations tossed in beneath by way of conclusion. I can't imagine a more entertaining, listener-friendly, or lucid summation.

Finales in Rondo Form

Symphony No. 68 in B-flat Major (1774–75)

Finale: Presto (CD 1, Track 12)
Scoring: 2 oboes, 2 bassoons, 2 horns, and strings

In order to understand what Haydn is up to in this finale, it's necessary to know a bit about the structure of the symphony as a whole. The heart of the work is its extraordinarily long adagio. With repeats, it lasts roughly fourteen minutes, or almost as long as all the other movements combined. For this reason, Haydn places the minuet second, giving listeners plenty of quick music before the epic slow section, after which he naturally needs a finale as colorful and varied as possible. The result is a particularly delightful and witty variation/rondo in the form ABAC(A1)D(A2)–coda, with a healthy dose of the concertante element besides.

The first episode (B, at 0:48) features the two bassoons, grunting humorously in their lowest register, after which the ritornello

(A) reappears unaltered. In the next episode (C, at 1:53), Haydn introduces the two oboes, playing a songful duet, leading to a variation of the ritornello (A1). The melody remains clearly audible, but the level of energy (already very high) increases even more. This spills over into an angry minor-key episode (D, at 3:24), which introduces a still more exciting variation of the ritornello (A2), with whirling violins and slashing chords in the orchestra.

The very funny coda immediately follows with a dramatic decrescendo, as the music suddenly seems to lose direction and comes to a dead halt. Solo strings and winds then play a mischievous, whispering game of "echo" (so marked in the score, at 4:41), each tossing about four notes of the ritornello, before the violins and then the entire orchestra recover and drive the symphony to its festive conclusion.

String Quartet in E-flat Major, Op. 33, No. 2 ("Joke") (1781)

Finale: Presto (CD 2, Track 7)

Here is the movement that gave the quartet its nickname, and I'm not going to spoil it for you by revealing the punch line in advance. The form is a classic rondo: ABACA–coda, and the ritornello theme has an extremely symmetrical shape very similar to the opening theme of Symphony No. 88's initial allegro: four phrases, the first three rhythmically identical, the last one a cadence. The joke depends entirely on the uneventful regularity of the movement's form, as well as on the rhythmic predictability of the theme. That's all you need know. Well, I'll give you one extra hint: the first phrase is a cadence too. When the coda begins at 2:55, try to guess when the music really ends.

Piano Trio No. 39 (25) in G Major (1795)

Finale: Rondo, in the Gypsies' Stile (Presto) (CD 2, Track 10)

In his late string quartets and symphonies, Haydn wrote no simple rondos, preferring instead some kind of sonata/rondo hybrid. However, in his late piano sonatas and trios, which he regarded as less weighty genres (most of the time), he usually kept to less complex forms while still filling them with all kinds of interesting material, often of an exotic or folklike character. This piece, written during his last months in London, gave his English audiences a taste of the Hungarian music that Haydn knew as well (or better) then any subsequent ethnomusicologist. As with the quartet finale just mentioned, the form is ABACA, without even an extended coda, and the Gypsy music appears in the two episodes (B and C), at 0:46 and 2:03 respectively. The ritornello theme itself, with its spiky accents and flashy piano writing, gives some hint of the fun to come.

Contrapuntal Finales

String Quartet in F Minor, Op. 20, No. 5 (1772)

Fuga a 2 soggetti (Fugue on 2 Subjects) (CD 2, Track 8)

Most people in the know would probably agree that no single group of works is more important in the history of its respective genre than Haydn's Op. 20 string quartets. Each of these six works is a distinctive masterpiece. Not least among their innovations is the fact that three of them end with fugues. In itself this was not new. Their novelty lies in the their rightness as conclusions to a sonata-style scheme, a function not just of Haydn's Bach-like mastery of counterpoint but of his similar

ability to make listeners forget all about the technical side and
focus solely on the music's expressive intensity. Without these
fugues, the quartets of everyone from Mozart to Beethoven to
Bartók would have been much different. No later composer has
escaped their influence.

This is the darkest and most serious in tone of the three Op.
20 fugues. Once again it's really necessary to hear the whole
quartet in order to truly understand why this must be so, but the
reason is not difficult to explain in words. The opening movement is largely sad, gently anxious, and it's followed by a more
energetic but still stern minuet. Haydn avoids major keys as the
basis of an entire movement until he comes to the adagio, which
is in fact another dance, a graceful siciliano with an elaborate
first violin part. This is one of Haydn's "spiritual" pieces. Under
the gentle, steady rhythm of the lower strings, the violin plays
an improvisational melodic line of such rapturous intensity that
its dreamy ecstasy becomes almost tactile. Haydn even indicates
that the player should break loose from the underlying tempo and
phrase as freely as possible.

After this heavenly vision, Haydn has two choices. He can
return to earth and continue in a vein similar to the first two
movements—or he can do what he does here: recognize that
after such a transfiguring experience, you may go home again tonally but not spiritually. As mentioned previously, the expressive
effect of pure counterpoint is rhetorical, like a discussion, rather
than a dramatic sequence of events, which is what the sonata style
is all about. This finale, then, is a meditation. Its tone is *sotto
voce*—that is, subdued—and having just glimpsed paradise, you
may hear in this dialogue on two simultaneous themes (subjects)
a sad and stoic acceptance of life in this "vale of tears." Haydn has
in fact found a finale that provides a satisfying emotional conclusion by returning to the home key, but because it is contemplative

rather than dramatic, it doesn't negate the impact of the adagio, which remains the expressive heart of the work.

Symphony No. 70 in D Major (1779)

Finale: Allegro con brio (CD 1, Track 16)
Scoring: flute, 2 oboes, bassoon, 2 horns, 2 trumpets, timpani,
*   and strings*

This symphony can be heard in many different ways. First, it expresses a basic conflict between the bright key of D major and a darkly moody D minor, since all its movements are in one or the other (or both). It also presents alternating *homophonic* (that is, melody plus accompaniment) and *polyphonic* (contrapuntal) textures. The first movement is in the expected sonata form, while the following andante is a set of alternating minor/major variations written as a canon in double counterpoint (which means the top and bottom parts switch places). A sturdy symphonic minuet then introduces a very eccentric and funny fugal finale.

As in Symphony No. 88, the heart of this piece lies in the slow movement. Both outer allegros are extremely concise. Unlike the later work, however, this finale does not resemble the first movement at all. Rather, its contrapuntal workings evoke the andante in style and texture, if not in melody. Haydn reinforces this metrically; the first and third movements are in 3/4, the second and forth in 2/4. As a summation of the entire work, this finale embodies the conflict between homophony and polyphony in the most amusing possible way, as well as the clash between minor and major modes. The opening consists of several alternations, first soft then loud, of five repeated notes answered by a three-note squiggle, a motive so pathetically primitive as to be laughable. It's not a tune as much as it is an "object," a bit of random musical stuff just lying around, casually picked up, and

given unaccountable prominence. Clearly this wisp of nothingness has little if any future. Or does it?

Suddenly, Haydn turns those five repeated notes (at 0:26) into
the initial motive of an enormous orchestral fugue, full of fantas-
tically intricate counterpoint, which rages on for pages of score.
As a reaction to the "nothing doing" opening, it's so extreme as
to appear outrageous, the musical equivalent of using a nuclear
weapon to squash a bug. The fugue vanishes as abruptly as it
began, and the opening returns (at 2:12), only now its single loud
outburst suggests a move from minor to major, an idea affirmed
in another brief but now triumphant passage of strenuous counterpoint. A few more of those primal initial motives nonchalantly
confirm the music's intention to stay put in its home key, and a
sudden fortissimo five-note shout has the final word, effectively
telling the fugue: "Stick that in your pipe!"

In most modern recordings, this symphony lasts less than
twenty minutes, and yet it packs quite a punch. One of the things
that undoubtedly attracted Haydn to counterpoint in the sonata
context is its vertical density and consequent ability to sound
large in a very small space. Subjectively speaking, this finale
seems to go on longer than a mere three minutes or so and thus
has the weight it needs to form a satisfying conclusion to the
whole work, while clearly retaining the lightness and energy
characteristic of most finales. You hear the same strategy when
you encounter the triple canon at the heart of Symphony No. 88's
closing sonata/rondo, and even more in Symphony No. 95, which
has a finale similar in concept to this one, although with a lengthy
and positively divine opening melody. In other words, Haydn uses
counterpoint to achieve a certain rhetorical power and grandeur,
but without ever risking long-windedness.

Finally, comparing this piece—which formally could actually
be described as a rondo in AB(A1)(B1)(A2) form—to the finale

of the String Quartet Op. 20, No. 5, you can hear that there is a real difference between a movement with a large polyphonic component and one that consists of counterpoint and little else. Haydn hasn't sacrificed any of the dramatic element by incorporating a fugue into this music. Just the opposite: by exaggerating the contrasts between sections as much as possible, he succeeds in characterizing the music even more boldly and, above all, amusingly.

Finales in Free Forms

String Quartet in C Major, Op. 54, No. 2 (1788)

Finale: Adagio (CD 2, Track 4)

One of the very few works in sonata style to end with an adagio, this extraordinary movement caps an equally exceptional quartet. Like Symphony No. 70, all its movements are in either the minor or major of its home key—in this case, C. What this means practically is not that the music is harmonically monotonous (in the literal meaning of the term!) It is in fact so tonally unstable that Haydn needs this basic framework within which to operate. In other words, the key of C functions less as "home" than as a sort of border or fence, the ropes around the ring that contain the struggle within. Without this constraint, the result would be chaos. You can hear this pretty clearly right from the outset, when the initial allegro announces the opening theme and immediately begins moving to distant and very startling, seemingly inexplicable tonal regions.

The minor-key slow movement is astonishing even for Haydn: it is a passacaglia, and above its repeated bass line (or theme in this case), the first violin plays a written-out improvisation on Gypsy music. There is nothing even remotely like it in the entire quartet literature (at least before Bartók). This nocturnal, hypnotic Hungarian rhapsody never actually ends. Instead, the minuet interrupts in a more hopeful major mode, but its trio section is tragic—truly poignant, even pained, and it denies even the usually solid and hearty dance movement its traditional stability and poise. This means that the finale will have its work cut out for it in establishing the piece's final return home, and Haydn keeps the listener in suspense about what will happen until the very last minute.

He does this in several ways. First, the finale itself opens with a short, slow introduction that Haydn repeats immediately, thus clearly marking its introductory character. This leads to the expectation that some kind of quick movement will follow. After all, how many slow introductions lead to slow movements? Instead, a serene adagio begins (at 1:11) in counterpoint between first violin and cello, the second violin and viola accompanying with softly pulsating chords. This melody flows on majestically through a minor-key variation (at 3:28), confirming that the movement really is, apparently, an adagio.

The moment this certainty seems established, a presto interlude breaks out (at 4:40): will the quartet in fact end swiftly after all? No. This quick music is too light, too slender, to furnish a satisfying conclusion this late in the game, and so it stops as quickly as it started. The introduction returns (at 5:36) and leads to a final reprise of the adagio's main theme, which calmly, soothingly, brings the quartet to a conclusion, resolving at last into silence. At a stroke, Haydn has traced an emotional journey that would find no parallel until the late romantic period: the work might best be described as a quest for peace, a search for refuge from mundane struggles and cares, and the idea of making the music's goal a slow, transfiguring finale was one that romantic composers of Mahler's generation at the turn of the twentieth century seized upon with particular enthusiasm.

Piano Sonata No. 60 (50) in C Major (1794)

Finale: Allegro molto (CD 2, Track 13)

Haydn being Haydn, it's but a short step from the sublime to the ridiculous, in the form of a finale that clearly makes fun of the "finale problem" itself. This sonata begins with one of his most elaborate first-movement sonata allegros; continues with a solemn, radiant adagio; and ends with a teeny, tiny, two-minute-long scherzo (a real one—not a fast minuet) so slender that it doesn't even have time for a trio. In fact, it's just the A section in its traditional two halves, both repeated—kind of. I say "kind of" because Haydn naturally has a few tricks up his sleeve.

As you have heard, the second half of most A sections of scherzos or minuets often consists of a mini–development section leading back more or less literally to the first half. Well, this particular example certainly tries to do just that, but it gets lost, hits wrong notes, hesitates, stumbles, finally slips into the right key (at 1:01), and celebrates the fact with indecent glee. Too short to be a "real" finale, but too naïve and innocent to know any better, Haydn asks the listener to accept this ending with the same affectionate indulgence that you might give to a child at a formal affair who hasn't learned proper manners but who still insists on being treated like a grownup. It's simply impossible not to smile and acquiesce.

This mischievous finale concludes a musical survey that has (so far) taken in one entire symphony and twenty-six individual movements. For all that, it barely scratches the surface. I have chosen these pieces, not just because they demonstrate the formal freedom and variety that characterize Haydn's work as a whole, but also in order to suggest that you can dig in just about anywhere to find something special and worth hearing. More importantly, Haydn's instrumental works all share in the formal solutions and innovations that his mastery of the sonata style made possible—so listen fearlessly, confidently, and trust the music to lead you unerringly down hundreds of characterful expressive paths just waiting to be explored.

Part 3

A Topical View

Vocal Works, Sacred and Secular

God in the heart and a good little woman on the arm;
one makes a man holy, the other keeps him warm.
>—text set by Haydn as a canon (round) and reused as the
"Et incarnatus est" (and was made man) section
of the Credo in his *Heiligmesse* (1797).

Sacred Music

Masses

No. 1 in G, possibly know as Missa "Rorate coeli desuper"
(early)

Scoring: strings, organ, mixed choir

No. 2 in F, Missa brevis (1749)

Scoring: strings, organ, 2 sopranos, mixed choir

No. 3 in C, Missa Cellensis in hon. BVM, also known as the
Cäcilienmesse (St. Cecilia Mass) (1766)

Scoring: 2 oboes, 2 bassoons, [2 horns], 2 trumpets, timpani,
strings, organ, soloists, mixed choir

No. 4 in D Minor, Missa "Sunt bona mixta malis" [fragment]
(1767)

No. 5 in E♭, Missa in honorem Beatissimae Virginis Mariae, also known as the Grosse Orgelmesse (Great Organ Mass) (c. 1768–74)

Scoring: 2 English horns, 2 horns, [2 trumpets, timpani], strings, organ, soloists, mixed choir

No. 6 in G, Missa Sancti Nicolai, Nicolaimesse (1772)

Scoring: 2 oboes, 2 horns, strings, organ, soloists, mixed choir

No. 7 in B♭, Missa brevis Sancti Joannis de Deo, also known as the Kleine Orgelmesse (Little Organ Mass) (c. 1775)

Scoring: strings, organ, soprano solo, mixed choir

No. 8 in C, Missa Cellensis, also known as the Mariazellermesse (1782)

Scoring: 2 oboes, bassoon, 2 trumpets, timpani, strings, organ, soloists, mixed choir

No. 9 in B♭, Missa sancti Bernardi von Offida, also known as the Heiligmesse (Holy Mass, for the quotation of an old religious melody in the Sanctus) (1796)

Scoring: 2 clarinets, 2 oboes, 2 bassoons, 2 trumpets, timpani, strings, organ, soloists, choir

No. 10 in C, Missa in tempore belli (Mass in Time of War), also known as the Paukenmesse (Timpani Mass) (1796)

Scoring: flute, 2 clarinets, 2 oboes, 2 bassoons, 2 horns, 2 trumpets, timpani, strings, organ, soloists, choir

No. 11 in D Minor, Missa in angustiis (Mass in Meager [literally, "Straitened"] Times), also known as the "Nelson Mass" (1798)

Scoring: 3 trumpets, timpani, strings, organ, soloists, mixed choir

No. 12 in B♭, Theresienmesse (named for the Empress Marie Therese) (1799)

Scoring: 2 clarinets, 2 trumpets, timpani, strings, organ, soloists, mixed choir

No. 13 in B♭, Schöpfungsmesse (Creation Mass) (1801)

Scoring: 2 clarinets, 2 oboes, 2 bassoons, 2 horns, 2 trumpets, timpani, strings, organ, soloists, mixed choir

No. 14 in B♭, Harmoniemesse (Wind-Band Mass) (1802)

Scoring: flute, 2 clarinets, 2 oboes, 2 bassoons, 2 horns, 2 trumpets, timpani, strings, organ, soloists, choir

Note: The solo vocalists in the Masses are usually the standard four—soprano, alto, tenor, and bass—but Haydn sometimes calls on additional voices for brief passages, so I have simply listed "soloists" generally rather than specifying the vocal parts in further detail.

Other Sacred Works

Stabat Mater (1767)

Scoring: 2 oboes, 2 English horns, strings, organ, soprano, alto, tenor, bass, mixed choir

The Seven Last Words (oratorio version) (1796)

Scoring: 2 flutes, 2 clarinets, 2 oboes, 2 bassoons, contrabassoon, 2 trumpets, 2 horns, 2 trombones, timpani, strings, soprano, alto, tenor, bass, mixed choir

The Creation (oratorio) (1798)

Scoring: 3 flutes, 2 clarinets, 2 oboes, 2 bassoons, contrabassoon, 2 trumpets, 2 horns, 3 trombones, timpani, strings, continuo (piano), soprano, tenor, bass, mixed choir

Te Deum in C Major (for the Empress Marie Therese) (1800)

Scoring: flute, 2 oboes, 2 bassoons, 3 trumpets, 2 horns, 3
trombones, timpani, strings, mixed choir

Sometime in 1801, the village of St. Johann near Plan, Bohemia, decided to produce Haydn's *The Creation* in their parish church. As a matter of form, they requested permission of the religious authorities in Prague, and it was surprisingly refused. The rector, Charles Ockl, an admirer of Haydn, consulted the citizenry, and it was decided to build a stage and perform the work outdoors. When this proved impossible, the townspeople decided to use the church anyway, and for this purpose they arranged a fake "kidnapping" of Ockl so that he, not being present, would not be held responsible. The local priest, however, took Haydn's name to be *Heiden,* which is German for "heathens." He made a point of denouncing from the pulpit in scathing terms the performance in his church of an oratorio by heathens. Ockl, afraid of losing his job, wrote to Haydn describing the whole imbroglio and received back the following response:

> Nobly born and most respected Sir!
>
> I have duly received your two letters of the 29th May and 5th July with which you favored me, and have noted their contents with pleasure. I was quite delighted to hear that my Oratorio was received by all the music-lovers in your district with the approbation which it has been fortunate enough to enjoy in almost the whole of Europe; but it was with considerable astonishment that I read of the curious happenings consequent on the performance, which happenings, considering the age in which we live, reflect but little credit on the intelligence and emotions of those responsible.
>
> The story of the creation has always been regarded as most sublime, and as one which inspires the utmost awe in mankind. To accompany this great occurrence with suitable music

could certainly produce no other effect than to heighten these sacred emotions in the heart of the listener, and so put him in a frame of mind where he is most susceptible to the kindness and omnipotence of the Creator, —And this exaltation of the most sacred emotions is supposed to constitute desecration of a church?

Have no fears about the outcome of this affair, for I am convinced that an intelligent consistory will learn a good deal from this apostle of peace and unity: it is not unlikely that the listeners went away from my Oratorio with their hearts far more uplifted than after hearing his sermons. No church has ever been desecrated by my Creation; on the contrary: the adoration and worship of the Creator, which it inspires, can be more ardently and intimately felt by playing it in such a sacred edifice.

If, however, this affair—which sounds completely ridiculous to every intelligent person—is not settled by the consistory, I am willing to place it before their Imperial and Royal Majesties, for Their Majesties have never heard this Oratorio without being deeply moved, and are quite convinced of the value of this sacred work. I am, Sir, most respectfully,

Your devoted servant,

Joseph Haydn
Doctor of Music (Landon 1978, 5:70–71)

Haydn's offer to take the matter up with the emperor and empress was no idle threat. Empress Marie Therese, one of the composer's biggest fans, had herself been soprano soloist in a performance of *The Creation* in Vienna (Haydn said that she had a weak voice). Still, this very funny episode highlights the most important issue that has dogged Haydn's sacred compositions in the scholarly literature at least since the late eighteenth century. Specifically, while everyone admits that they contain great music considered purely on that basis, some question whether they are not too theatrical and secular in tone to be considered great *litur-*

gical music—as if musicologists are in a position to pass judgment on behalf of the community of the faithful for whom Haydn was writing. The fact is that these believers, plus countless others of all persuasions over more than two centuries, have always found—as Haydn would have put it—their hearts receptive to his vivid musical embodiment of their "sacred emotions."

That said, there's no point in gilding the lily: Haydn's religious works, whether for the church or the concert hall, have all the qualities of his music generally. In other words, they are entertaining, exciting, and surprising, and so it's easy to understand how those with a more penitential (not to say self-lacerating) view of religious devotion might be offended and even feel guilty for having such a good time listening to them. Haydn was aware of this problem. His attitude, he asserted, was that "God doesn't condemn those he created from dust for being dust." If the good Lord gave him talent as well as a basically cheerful and humorous disposition, then sacred music partaking of this inner nature would hardly be offensive to the only ears that ultimately mattered come Judgment Day. Thus, you can find in all of Haydn's religious works that wonderful Enlightenment-era celebration of—and pride in—humanity as the crown of creation, despite its inherent sinfulness, weaknesses, and foibles. This is music that has nothing to prove. Haydn takes the fundamental tenets of Catholic belief as given, and all that remains for him is to do his very best work as a composer.

Haydn had a very good reason for turning exclusively to vocal music, mostly sacred, at the end of his life, refusing to write any more symphonies. It's the same logic that caused Bach to assemble the B Minor Mass in his twilight years as well. In an era when there was no such thing as "classical music," only what was in fashion at any given time, Haydn clearly and consciously understood that most of his instrumental output would not likely survive changing tastes and continued artistic progress. On the other hand, he had seen in England the great Handel festivals and the beginnings of the classical music culture as we know it today. This is why he wrote his two oratorios, *The Creation* and *The Seasons,* both of which he modestly assumed would "probably" survive. It also explains why he wrote his last six Masses. They were, first and foremost, a bid at immortality, achieved by uniting music of supreme quality with the ageless truths of an eternal text.

In the end, Haydn's gambit worked. For generations after his death, until the mid–twentieth century, his instrumental music (save for a few quartets and couple of symphonies) languished unappreciated and unperformed. But his great choral works, the oratorios and Masses, remained staples of the repertoire in German-speaking countries, heard both in concert and in church. They kept his name alive until the resurgence of interest in him took hold in the world at large, just a handful of decades ago. So Haydn's critics had a point in one sense: the late Masses are every bit as much "about" him and his music as they are about the liturgy. They are romantic works, subjective in tone and technique—one man's defining statement about his art and his faith. At the same time, as with all great fusions of words and music, they are extremely sensitive to the meaning of the text as well as mindful of past precedents, however radically Haydn reinterprets them.

Perhaps the most famous example of his habit of intertwining the sacred and secular occurs in the *Mass in Time of War* (Haydn's own title), where the solo timpani in the Agnus Dei section chillingly represent the advance of distant armies, above which the choir's cries for mercy achieve an unheard of degree of dramatic (and realistic) motivation. It was a sound that resonated not just with contemporary audiences but with Beethoven, who borrowed the same idea in his *Missa solemnis,* and which continues to influence composers to the present day (the most famous modern example being Britten's *War Requiem*). Indeed, after this work, sacred music would never be the same again.

The ensuing prayer of "Dona nobis pacem" (Give us peace) also loses its traditional associations, in this case with gentle pastoral imagery. Haydn sees it as a demand, not a request, with peace achieved through victory in battle, a triumph of good over the forces of evil. In fact all of Haydn's big Masses end in a festive spirit of confidence, overflowing with optimism. This is the logical outcome of his treating the text as a rich tapestry of emotions in which feelings of ecstatic spirituality commingle with the joys and sorrows of physical mortality. The music thus celebrates our humanity as a glorious earthly manifestation of the Divine, and this in turn renders the technical (and somewhat arbitrary) distinction between "sacred" and "secular" moods expressively irrelevant. However much purists may carp, in Haydn's hands, the Mass gains an emotional immediacy and communicative power that has not diminished one bit over the intervening centuries. Paradoxically, and as so often happens with great art, the timeliness of the setting has assured the timelessness of the results.

Still another testament to Haydn's ongoing rethinking of the relationship between text and music concerns his settings of the words "Benedictus qui venit in nomine Domini" (Blessed is he who comes in the name of the Lord). This is often a gentle meditation emphasizing the idea of "blessedness." In the late Masses, however, Haydn seizes on the many possible ways of "coming." The *Wind-Band Mass* (No. 14), for example, sets these words as a breathless scherzo, full of nervous anticipation. His last completed work, the energy and originality of this music would be astonishing in a man half his age. The *Creation Mass*, on the other hand, offers a very earthy country-dance, a sort of apotheosis of Haydn's folk-music style and the very embodiment of pastoral innocence and grace. In the "Nelson Mass," you encounter a solemn march—measured, threatening, and ultimately overwhelming, with blaring trumpets and pounding drums. This latter work is extraordinary in many other respects as well, not least for its virile yet gaunt scoring (three trumpets, timpani, strings, and solo organ) and its manic emotional range.

You can hear this very clearly on CD 2, track 17, which contains the opening movement, the Kyrie, whose simple text of "Kyrie eleison, Christe eleison, Kyrie eleison" (Lord have mercy, Christ have mercy, Lord have mercy) Haydn sets in a beautiful example of his late sonata style. The first subject, an anguished D minor lament, features acid chords on the organ, slashing strings, and menacing trumpets and timpani. The rhythm in these last instruments (dum, dadadum, dum, dum) is one of Haydn's personal fingerprints, found throughout his orchestral works from the First Symphony onwards. The chorus enters with desperate cries of "Kyrie eleison," followed by the soprano's solo entreaty (at 0:46).

The second subject of this sonata-form movement is, not surprisingly, the clause "Christe eleison." With a shockingly sudden change of key to the major, a contrast typical of the work's often violent mood swings, the soprano sings an elaborate coloratura line that beautifully expresses the happiness Haydn feels whenever his thoughts turn to the humanity and mercy of Jesus Christ. This is a constant in his sacred music, and it also explains the explosion of joy that will conclude the Mass in about forty minutes' time. The movement's development section belongs to the chorus and contains a fugato based on a fragment of the opening Kyrie (at 1:27).

This leads gradually to a recapitulation (at 2:38), the opening of which is beyond thrilling. Haydn combines the chorus's lament with the soprano's soaring Christe coloratura in the home key of D minor. It sends a shiver down the spine, while not incidentally recapitulating both first and second subjects simultaneously. As always, formal and expressive strokes of genius work hand in hand. Further expansion and development of the turbulent Kyrie music bring the movement to its sternly energetic conclusion. The title, "Nelson Mass," was given to the piece in 1800 when it was performed in honor of Admiral Nelson's visit to the Prince and Princess Esterházy. Aside from defeating Napoleon's navy, the admiral was a big admirer of Haydn and supposedly was so impressed by what he heard that he asked the composer for the pen he had used to compose the work.

Haydn wrote Masses of many different types, from tiny short services (*Missa brevis*), such as Nos. 2 and 7, to grand "cantata Masses" lasting more than an hour (No. 3), in which the various sections are carved up into arias and choruses, as in Bach's famous work in B minor and Mozart's magnificent, incomplete setting in C minor. But the rest of Haydn's Masses are "symphonic," in that each major section—Kyrie, Gloria, Credo, Sanctus, Agnus— increasingly encompasses a single sweeping movement, perhaps with one or two contrasting sections. The last six Masses, in particular, bring this process to its logical conclusion: they take thirty-five to forty minutes each and are truly vocal symphonies in all but name, applying the same formal techniques of sonata- style construction that you find in the instrumental works. They set the standard for all future works in the form, from Beethoven to Bruckner and beyond.

The same symphonic principles apply to the construction of *The Creation,* Haydn's glorious retelling of the Genesis story, despite the usual division into distinct arias and choruses. There are, in fact, only five solo numbers in the entire work. The remaining pieces blend the soloists with the choir (and each other) and create excitement in the same way that Haydn does in the purely instrumental compositions, although here the expressive color of the music is appropriately always governed by the sense of the text. For example, in the concluding chorus of part 1, "The Heavens Are Telling" (CD 2, track 15), note how the mood darkens when the trio of archangels speaks of night in their first episode (at 0:28).

> *Chorus:*
> The heavens are telling the glory of God,
> The firmament displays the wonder of his works.
>
> *Trio (Gabriel, Uriel, Raphael):*
> To day that is coming speaks it the day,
> The night that is gone, to following night.
>
> *Chorus:*
> The heavens are telling, etc.
>
> *Trio:*
> In all the land resounds the word,
> Never unperceived, ever understood.
>
> *Chorus:*
> The heavens are telling, etc.

If this movement were a piece of instrumental music, you would recognize it immediately as a rondo by virtue of its ABACA form. The final appearance of A broadens out into a brilliant choral fugue, and so the entire number (although more concise owing to the brief text) actually has a shape very similar to the finale of the "Clock" Symphony (No. 101), which is a sonata/rondo with the final appearance of the ritornello similarly becoming the subject of a fugue. There is absolutely nothing contrived in any of this, as you can hear for yourself by following the words (incidentally, both of Haydn's oratorios were published with both English and German texts). The drama and continuity of the sonata style support vocal writing just as well as they do instrumental music. Mozart proved this in his operas, and Haydn does the same in his Masses and oratorios.

The Creation remains the most popular oratorio in the repertoire after Handel's *Messiah,* and it confirmed Haydn's stature as the greatest living composer of his day. Other important sacred concert works include his darkly expressive, early setting of the *Stabat Mater,* the largest musical arrangement of that prayer before Dvořák's and a work often strikingly similar in mood and even theme to Mozart's Requiem (compare the former's tenor aria "Vidit suum" to the latter's choral "Lacrimosa"). There's also the oratorio version of the *Seven Last Words [of the Savior on the Cross]* and the incredibly powerful Te Deum for Empress Marie Therese (his second setting of that text, and one that clearly influenced Bruckner's). This last work opens with a snatch of chant that in Haydn's hands becomes as catchy and elemental as a college fight-song.

With only those two later exceptions of Dvořák and Bruckner, Haydn was actually the last great composer to devote a substantial portion of his output to the Catholic liturgy, and his legacy remains unsurpassed—as well as hugely underappreciated in the critical literature—to this day. Neither the fact that we live in a more secular age nor the sectarian divide that still prejudices some commentators against music composed for a specific church should blind us to the depth of emotion, spirituality, and musical mastery that Haydn's religious pieces reveal. They are incredibly moving, passionately sincere works; their expressive qualities are universal, communicating independently of any specific creed.

Secular Music

Operas

L'infedeltà delusa (Infidelity Deceived) (1773)

*Scoring: 2 oboes, 2 horns, 2 bassoons, timpani, strings,
          continuo (harpsichord for the simple [dry] recitatives),
          2 sopranos, 2 tenors, bass*

L'isola disabitata (The Desert Island) (1779)

*Scoring: flute, 2 oboes, bassoon, 2 horns, timpani, strings,
    continuo, 2 sopranos, tenor, bass*

La fedeltà premiata (Fidelity Rewarded) (1780)

*Scoring: flute, 2 oboes, bassoon, 2 horns, 2 trumpets, timpani,
    strings, continuo, 4 sopranos, 2 tenors, 2 basses*

Armida (1783)

*Scoring: flute, 2 oboes, 2 clarinets, 2 bassoons, 2 horns,
    2 trumpets, timpani, strings, continuo, 2 sopranos,
    2 tenors, bass*

Orfeo ed Euridice (1791)

*Scoring: 2 flutes, 2 oboes, 2 clarinets, 2 English horns,
    2 bassoons, 2 horns, 2 trumpets, 2 trombones, timpani,
    harp, strings, continuo, 2 sopranos, tenor, bass, mixed
    choir*

This is not the place to launch a ringing, blow-by-blow defense of Haydn's operas. Everyone agrees that they contain magnificent music. The only issue is if and when this will finally be recognized by the public at large. Haydn himself was proud of them, and even though he was quick to yield the operatic stage to Mozart and acknowledge him as the greatest opera composer of his age, as one who produced and conducted hundreds of operas in the 1770s and 80s, he not only knew the competition as well as anyone but surely also understood what it would take to do better. Given the fact that no one cares today about any of Haydn's non-Mozartean contemporaries (except Gluck), it's safe to assume that he did indeed do better, particularly as, with one exception, all of Haydn's operas predate Mozart's first great comedy, *The Marriage of Figaro.*

Certainly the audible evidence supports this. Now that the history of opera no longer effectively begins with Mozart, and baroque opera has come roaring back into favor along with many of Mozart's less-than-interesting early stage-works as well, it's entirely possible that the best of Haydn's ten or so surviving operas could undergo a positive reappraisal. Until then, you may see in the literature more than a few very silly comments about them, ranging from the usual generic criticism of their librettos to such strange formulations as "Haydn's style was too dramatic for opera," or "he was incapable of adapting himself to the pace of staged drama." The most damaging and inapplicable criticism of all stems from drawing the wrong conclusions from Haydn's own statement about his operas being too dependent on local circumstances to be suitable for presentation elsewhere.

This may have been true in the 1880s, but from today's point of view, this comment, taken without qualification, would be equally applicable to all of Haydn's music, and Mozart's, and Beethoven's. Contingent factors are only relevant to the extent that they had a demonstrable negative impact on the finished product, and Haydn was talking about the effect of works tailored for one audience when performed before another with different expectations, and not issues of absolute musical quality per se. What seems far more likely is that he realized, after the pleasure of his initial encounter with Mozart, that his career was unlikely to offer him the opportunity to work on a similar scale, and so he simply preferred to stop unless he found conditions more to his liking.

The five works listed are not, in fact, completely unknown. They have all been recorded more than once, and by major artists. Typically, they cover a very wide range of styles, making the very idea of "Haydn opera" as an undifferentiated lump a dubious proposition. Take, for example, *L'isola disabitata,* a delightful work in two short acts (lasting about ninety minutes) that contains no simple (dry) recitative at all. Completely through-composed and swiftly moving, like the famous "reform operas" of Gluck but with a much higher degree of symphonic integration, it is unique. The plot deftly mixes sad and comic elements, while the focus remains squarely on the human drama concerning its four principals. The story describes the rescue, from the desert island of the title, of an embittered wife and her baby sister by the husband—and his handsome young companion—who she believes abandoned them there (they were actually kidnapped by pirates while the two women were freshening up).

Of the two comedies in the list, *L'infedeltà delusa*—with its pastoral subject, funny situations, and theatrically effective two-act structure (lasting barely two hours)—has proven successful in modern revivals. *La fedeltà premiata* is more ambitious and contains some of Haydn's finest music from the late 1770s. Its electrifying overture became the famous "hunting" finale of Symphony No. 73 "La chasse." Indeed, it seems that quite a few of Haydn's symphonies of the late 1770s and early 80s borrowed music from his stage works. The only real problem with this opera from a dramatic point of view, as with Mozart's early comedies, stems from the strange three-act structure in which everything happens in the long first two acts, while the brief third part serves as a kind of appendix or quick wind-up. Once past this hurdle, that initial pair of acts turn out to be magnificent, with symphonically structured finales highly suggestive of Mozart's later work (indeed, the opera was successful in Vienna in 1784, and it has been suggested that Mozart knew it and may have learned from it).

The revival of baroque *opera seria* has given Haydn's (and Mozart's) serious operas a potential new audience as well. Works of this type concern larger-than-life characters, usually caught in a conflict between love and duty. They don't evolve over the course of the work (or at least not much), and each represents a particular archetype: the hero, the despairing heroine, the vengeful jilted lover, the traitor, the noble monarch, and so forth. The arias encapsulate fixed emotional states, while the action takes place in the recitatives. Haydn's *Armida* largely follows this pattern, save that he makes a deliberate and very successful effort to humanize the pagan sorceress Armida and the crusading knight Rinaldo. Several famous sopranos have found in the female lead a superb portrait of a woman in love and later scorned, and the music, particularly of the final scenes, is spectacular.

Orfeo ed Euridice, Haydn's last opera, was written while he was in England, but owing to political machinations (so what else is new?), it was never performed. For many years it was believed to be fragmentary, but modern scholarship has assembled what appears to be the complete score. It was played for the first time only in the 1950s, in a production featuring no less than the young Maria Callas. The dazzling act 3 aria for the character of Genio (a sibyl), "Al tuo seno fortunato" (To your happy breast), contains some of the most thrilling soprano coloratura this side of Mozart's "Queen of the Night" from *The Magic Flute*. The tragic ending, with Orpheus ripped to pieces by the Bacchantes exactly as in the Greek myth, is exceptionally powerful stuff, and once again the opera's four acts last only a bit more than two hours. So even if Haydn isn't an opera composer on the level of Mozart, he certainly is one on the level of Haydn, with his own voice and expressive language, and God knows that ought to be enough to gain these works a fair hearing.

Other Secular Vocal Works

Arianna a Naxos (cantata for soprano and piano) (1789)

Scena di Berenice (concert aria for soprano and orchestra) (1795)
Scoring: flute, 2 oboes, 2 clarinets, 2 bassoons, 2 horns, strings

English Canzonettas (Songs) for Voice and Piano (1794–95)

First Series: "The Mermaid's Song," "Recollection," "Pastoral
Song," "Despair," "Pleasing Pain," "Fidelity"
Second Series: "Sailor's Song," "The Wanderer," "Sympathy,"
"She never told her love," "Piercing Eyes," "Transport of
Pleasure [Content]"
Individual Songs: "The Spirit's Song," "O Tuneful Voice"

The Seasons (oratorio) (1801)

*Scoring: piccolo, 2 flutes, 2 oboes, 2 clarinets, 2 bassoons,
contrabassoon, 4 horns, 3 trumpets, 3 trombones,
timpani, triangle, tambourine, strings, continuo
(piano), soprano, tenor, bass, mixed choir*

Arianna a Naxos
Scena di Berenice

Both of these works offer graphic, opera seria–style portraits
of a woman in extremis, and for the same reason: each has been
deserted (although in different ways) and faces life alone, without the man that she loves. In *Arianna a Naxos,* the story is the
familiar one from Greek myth, in which the heroine runs the
gamut from misery to rage at her abandonment by Theseus on
the island Naxos. The piano accompaniment is also richly elabo-
rated and expressively conceived, while the sequence of recitatives and arias makes this twenty-minute piece a true emotional
tour-de-force at vocal recitals and a brilliant display item for the
soprano. Haydn never realized his intention to orchestrate this
work, but it exists in a contemporary version for string orchestra
in which he may have had a hand, as well as in later arrangements
for larger forces.

In the *Scena di Berenice,* a lengthy accompanied recitative out-
lines the initial situation: Berenice laments the death of her lover,

begging his shade (in a moving, slow lament) to take her with him to the underworld. Another brief recitative leads to a swift, agitated conclusion in which she begs for death. It's impossible to listen to this piece and have any doubt that Haydn was in any way unfit for opera or had difficulties in expressing tragic emotions. A passionate, desperate work, it inspired Beethoven to write his own famous concert aria "Ah! perfido" a year later.

English Canzonettas

It's not often mentioned, but Haydn basically invented what is now called the "art song," which in his own day was something new: a high-quality popular song for domestic consumption by the nascent middle class. The most famous composer working in this genre was Schubert, a full three generations younger, and Haydn is the only one of the great Viennese triumvirate of classical-period composers who devoted significant time to song composition. He wrote about fifty of them in all (not counting the hundreds of folk-song arrangements he either made personally or supervised), most published in sets of six or twelve, along with some important single works besides (such as the "Emperor's Hymn" that became the Austrian national anthem). By general consent, the English Canzonettas represent his finest achievement in the genre, and while hardly as well known as they should be, they have never entirely vanished from the repertoire.

In fact one of them, "Pastoral Song," perhaps better known by the text of its opening line, "My mother bids me bind my hair," became so ubiquitous that it might be mistaken for an anonymous folk song. I knew it as a child, for example, long before I discovered that Haydn was the man that wrote it. Most of the texts are by Anne Hunter, another of Haydn's lady friends, but they also include settings of Shakespeare ("She never told her love"), as well as English translations of Metastasio. The two individual pieces, "O Tuneful Voice" and "A Spirit's Song," rank among the most profoundly moving settings before Schubert. These late works, Haydn's earlier German songs (which he performed himself), as well as the German part-songs that he composed after his return to Vienna, reveal a highly developed lyrical gift and the all-important ability—like Schubert—to capture the mood of the text in just a few bars of music. They are little gems.

The Seasons

Haydn famously called the libretto of *The Seasons* "Frenchified trash" and claimed that the effort required to make something great out of it cost him years of his life. Most listeners would agree that the time spent was worth it, even if the result has never been as popular as the *The Creation,* perhaps owing to the decidedly secular nature of the subject. Still, there's something fitting in Haydn ending his career (save for his last two Masses) with a pastoral celebration of nature, simple pleasures, and the eternal cycle of life.

In *The Creation,* Haydn indulged his gift for musical description, not just of chaos leading to the appearance of light, but also of the advent of God's creatures (man and animals both). In order to make all this vivid, he used his large orchestra to the fullest, and these sections have always been particular highlights. Haydn, to be honest, was of two minds about them. As noted in connection with the symphonies, he had no problem with tone painting as long as he believed that the subject matter was inherently musical. The text of *The Seasons* pushed the boundaries of what he considered suitable to the very limits. For example, the suggestion that he include such sound effects as the croaking of frogs annoyed him, although he followed the text faithfully and, I suspect, with more than a touch of guilty enjoyment. He was incredibly good at this sort of thing. The drunken harvest festival at the end of "Autumn" that Haydn feared might sound too realistically vulgar stands as one of the score's greatest moments (at least to modern ears), as does music's first, really graphic storm sequence in "Summer."

In the end, posterity has approved of Haydn's handling of the material, however intractable it may have seemed to him at the time, and has lauded his willingness to pull out all the orchestral stops and outdo himself in the lavish application of instrumental color. The piece truly is a summing up of all that he could do as composer for voices and orchestra, masterfully scored for an ensemble of a size and variety that would not be seen again for something like three decades. Ironically, this is the most serious mark against the work. There's so much eventful music packed into its four parts that the piece is often described as intimidatingly long and taxing. Such rumors have always been greatly exaggerated.

The truth turns about to be surprising: the oratorio is actually gratifyingly compact. Its four parts play for only five or ten minutes over two hours, or just a handful of minutes more than *The Creation*'s three parts. In total time, *The Seasons* is a good quarter hour shorter than a complete performance of Handel's *Messiah,* and it knocks a solid sixty-plus minutes off the average timing of Bach's *St. Matthew Passion*. It just sounds huge: that's part of its secret. It remains a world unto itself. Each of its four parts runs the entire gamut of expression. The arias are given to a trio of country folk—Lucas, Simon, and Jane—while the choruses are tremendously varied and often spectacular. Haydn sets each season as if in a single, sweeping gesture, and the music's energy defies description.

You really have to hear it to understand this last point, so I offer on CD 2, track 16, the thrilling hunting chorus from "Autumn." Haydn peppers this number with the actual horn calls that signaled the progress of the chase to participants strung out over the countryside on horseback. Some of these tunes may sound familiar to you even today, and as late as the 1920s, you could still hear one of them (at 3:29) in Italian composer Ottorino Respighi's tone poem *Feste Romane* (Roman Festivals). Lucas introduces the chorus with an accompanied recitative describing scampering rabbits rounded up for the slaughter, and as always in these cases (in *The Creation* also), the musical description comes first, the verbal explanation afterwards. When Lucas's brief narration concludes, the horns blast in with their first call, and the hunt is on. The orchestration includes trombones but omits trumpets and timpani entirely, giving the piece a lightness and bounce to the rhythm that really does capture the spirit of the chase.

> *Lucas (recitative):*
> Here closed rings compel
> The timid hares to quit their haunts.
> From ev'ry side they're driven in,
> And now here is escape,
> They wheel and wind, but fall
> And soon in showy files
> Display'd they lie.
>
> *Chorus of Countrymen and Hunters:*
> Hear! Hear! The clank and noise
> That makes the forest ring!
> It is the shrilling sound of horns!
> The barking of greedy hounds!
> Here starts the fear-aroused stag;
> Behind runs the pack and the hunters crew.
> He flies! He flies! O see, what strains!
> Behind runs the pack and the hunters crew.
> O see, what bounds!
> Lo there! the copse and thicket he bursts.
> And skims o'er the fields to the deepest wood.

Now has he deceived the hounds.
Dispers'd they ramble and stray about.
Dispers'd are the hounds.
Tayo, halloo, Tayo!
The hunters voice, the piercing horn
Have brought the pack again.
Ho! Ho! Ho! Tayo! Ho! Ho!
With ardour increased,
Rashly pours along
In the track the rejoined gang.
Hallo! Tayo! Halloo!
Surrounded now from ev'ry side,
His spirits and vigor lost,
Exhausted drops the nimble deer.
His gasping agony proclaim of sounding brass,
The conqu'ring tune of hunters, the loud triumphant shouts,
'Tis done: his final doom proclaim,
Halali, halali!

And so this brief survey of Haydn's vocal music draws to a close on what I hope you agree is a very high note indeed. Even if history has decided that he will be remembered primarily as a composer of instrumental works, to ignore these pieces is to miss an extremely important aspect of Haydn's talent, personality, and creative spirit, not to mention a whole slew of outright masterpieces. If you are building a Haydn collection, I would suggest you consider getting to know *The Creation, The Seasons,* and a couple of the last six Masses, in any order that suits you, and then broaden your listening experience as time permits. You can count on all the music described here to share the same high quality that characterizes Haydn's nonvocal works, making it a very safe bet and a guaranteed ticket to enjoyment.

Solitary Masterworks

Concerning his own works Haydn said, "sunt mala mixta bonis; there are some good children, and some bad children, and every so often a changeling has snuck in among them."

—G. A. Griesinger

This chapter deals with a dozen of those "changelings" that Haydn mentions above: some very well known, others obscure, all in fields for which he is not otherwise recognized as a major contributor. They are pretty uniformly wonderful, and their place in the ongoing series of ironies that constitutes Haydn's contemporary reputation is defined by the fact that when a composer writes tons of pieces in one genre, his output must be "uneven," but when he also writes single works in other genres, then the results are just as often described as "atypical" or "unidiomatic." The following brief discussions offer you the opportunity to listen and draw your own conclusions.

Five Concertos

Cello Concerto in C Major (1761–65)

Cello Concerto in D Major (1783)

Piano Concerto No. 6 in D Major, Hob. VIII:11 (1784)

All of the above scored for 2 oboes, 2 horns and strings

Trumpet Concerto in E-flat Major (1796)

Scoring: 2 flutes, 2 oboes, 2 bassoons, 2 horns, 2 trumpets, timpani, and strings

Sinfonia Concertante

Scoring: flute, 2 oboes, 2 bassoons, 2 horns, 2 trumpets, timpani, and strings (of which 1 oboe, 1 bassoon, 1 violin, and 1 cello play solo)

Haydn wrote many concertos, most of them very early works. It was a medium in which he seldom gave of his very best. There was something in Haydn's character that resisted the kind of fixed, structured dialogue represented by the opposition between the orchestra and a single soloist—at least as compared with the multicolored exchanges available to an orchestra in which different voices lead at different times. It was exactly this clear definition of roles that appealed to Mozart, making him the greatest concerto composer (especially for piano) who ever lived. Interestingly, Haydn's best concertos were—with the exception of the Piano Concerto in D Major—all written for instruments, or combinations of instruments, ignored by Mozart. As a result, they are uniformly important—indeed, landmark—works in the history of the form.

The two cello concertos, for example are the first "modern" pieces still in the repertoire of today's virtuoso cellists. Amazingly, the earlier of them was only rediscovered in 1961. It is a major work by any standard, with an incredibly exciting finale. Both concertos, in fact, are brilliantly written and quite difficult for the soloist. Unfortunately, the D major piece for many years was played in a bowdlerized version that made its very long first movement (about twelve minutes) sound even longer than it should, but recent performances based on historical practice—with their lively tempos, sharper rhythms, and more vigorous accents—reveal the work to be much more interesting that previously supposed.

There are some serious authentication issues concerning Haydn's works for keyboard and orchestra, even before considering what instrument he actually wrote them for. Some are organ concertos, others clearly require the harpsichord, and the later ones sound best on piano. The D Major Concerto has one of Haydn's most famous finales, a delicious "Hungarian Rondo" similar to the "Rondo, in the Gypsies' Stile" for Piano Trio that you heard in chapter 8 (CD 2, track 10). This is his only piano concerto that withstands comparison to Mozart's finest work. Note the date: it was written just at the time that Haydn first met the young genius, and he composed no keyboard concertos thereafter.

Haydn's famous Trumpet Concerto is unarguably the finest ever written. It is also his very last orchestral work, one that fittingly reveals him conquering new territory up to the very end. Among the many wonders packed into its amazingly concise fifteen-or-so minutes, the slow movement reveals the trumpet as a lyrical, songful instrument for the first time in musical history, while the ritornello theme of the rondo finale would make just about everyone's list of Ten Greatest Tunes of the Classical Era. Trust me: you've heard it before. Note how the last appearance of this glorious melody takes on the same autumnal glow (the result of Haydn's using "subdominant harmony," if you want to get technical) that you can hear at the end of the andante of the "Surprise" Symphony.

The *Sinfonia Concertante* is one of only two such really great works from the classical period still in the repertoire today, the other being Mozart's piece for violin and viola (K. 364). *Concertante* simply means "concerto-like," and together these two works define the parameters of the medium. Mozart's is a true concerto for two soloists—today it would be called a "double concerto"—while Haydn's is clearly a three-movement symphony with four important leading voices highlighted (violin, oboe, bassoon, and cello). You have already heard (on CD 1, track 14) a sample of Haydn's earliest works in this hybrid form, which he simply called "symphonies": the trio "Morning, Noon, and Night" (Nos. 6–8).

This particular piece was composed in 1792, during the first London visit, as part of Haydn's ongoing competition with the rival concert series headed by his pupil Pleyel. The music has all the wit and wisdom of Haydn's famous "London" symphonies, and you may even sometimes see it listed as "Symphony No. 105." He had, in any case, long ago absorbed the concerto idea into his conception of symphonies, many of which truly are "concertos for orchestra" in the best sense of the term. This particular work had an important influence on twentieth-century Czech composer Bohuslav Martinů, who heard it played in Paris in 1930 and so admired its "perfection and simplicity" that he wrote his own *sinfonia concertante* for exactly the same solo forces in 1948.

The *Seven Last Words* (original orchestral version) (1785)

*Scoring: 2 flutes, 2 oboes, 2 bassoons, 4 horns, 2 trumpets,
          timpani, and strings*

Haydn wrote this compelling and truly unique masterpiece for the Good Friday service in Cadiz, Spain. It was, as Haydn learned at second hand, an impressive event. The church was draped in black and illuminated by candles, and after the priest spoke a sermon on each of the "last words" (phrases, really), the orchestra played a slow movement as an aid to personal meditation. The original commission called for Haydn to produce seven adagios lasting ten minutes each, but he himself admitted that he could not keep to this restriction without tiring his listeners, particularly as he clearly intended the piece to be heard independently, as a unified cycle. Most of the movements, or "sonatas," are in fact a touch shorter, but he added both an introduction and the concluding "earthquake," so once again one notes that musical contrast and sustaining interest always remain paramount considerations.

It is fascinating to see how Haydn met the challenge of writing so much slow music in sequence, for what turned out to be his longest single orchestral work of any kind:

Introduction: Maestoso ed Adagio
Scoring: 2 oboes, 2 bassoons, 2 horns, and strings

Sonata I: Largo
Pater, dimitte illis, quia nesciunt, quid faciunt
Father, forgive them, for they know not what they do
Scoring: as above

Sonata II: Grave e cantabile
Hodie mecum eris in Paradiso
Today shalt thou be with me in paradise
Scoring: 2 oboes, 2 bassoons, 4 horns, and strings

Sonata III: Grave
Mulier, ecce filius tuus
Woman, behold thy son
Scoring: 1 flute, 2 oboes, 2 bassoons, 2 horns, and strings

Sonata IV: Largo
Deus meus, Deus meus, utquid dereliquisti me?
My God, My God, why hast Thou forsaken me?
Scoring: as in Sonata II

Sonata V: Adagio
Sitio
I thirst
Scoring: 2 flutes, 2 oboes, 2 bassoons, 2 horns, and strings

Sonata VI: Lento
Consummatum est
It is finished
Scoring: as in Sonata III

Sonata VII: Largo
In manus tuus, Domine, commendo spiritum meum
Lord, into Thy hands I commend my spirit
Scoring: As in Sonata V (with violins muted)

"The Earthquake": Presto e con tutta la forza
Scoring: I flute, 2 oboes, 2 bassoons, 2 horns, 2 trumpets, timpani,
and strings

The first thing to note is that the melody of each sonata is shaped by the Latin text, although the actual words are not sung—true even of "Sitio" ("I thirst"), where the melody consists of a broken chain of two-note descending sequences played by the winds over a "dry" pizzicato accompaniment in the violins. This is program music, then, although what is being described is not so much an object or a story as it is an emotional state suggested by the appropriate biblical phrase. Everything about the work's large-scale structure suggests an emotional progression from darkness and despair to light and peace (framed by the introduction and the thunderous conclusion).

Haydn achieves this progression, fascinatingly, not by making some movements faster than the required adagio but by making them even slower. As you can see, there is in fact only a single adagio among the seven sonatas. A largo tempo characterizes the three most important emotional outcries of the dying Savior: the plea to forgive his oppressors, his moment of utter despair, and his final reconciliation with God. The remaining sonatas in the work's first half are the two slowest; those in the second half are the quickest. Note also the first appearance of the flute in Sonata III, in association with the person of the Virgin Mary. After the tragic climax of Sonata IV, this consoling timbre returns in the remaining three movements as a symbol of Christ's gradual acceptance of death and the reunion of his spirit with God the Father.

All this is shattered by the concluding earthquake, with its remarkable triple-forte conclusion, but this too has a purpose: to bring the listeners back to reality by offering a shocking change of perspective—from that of being an actual participant in the emotional journey of Christ on the cross to becoming once again a mere spectator, an outsider. It is a contrast that hammers home the otherworldly depth of the previous hour's music with exceptional force. Indeed, this work is critical as the proving ground for those spiritual qualities found in so many of Haydn's instrumental adagios generally, a truth that audiences of his day recognized immediately.

So compelling is the music's message, in fact, that this unlikely piece became one of Haydn's most popular works, and it remains so, although curiously not in its original version. Aside from turning it into an oratorio by adding a chorus, soloists, heavier orchestration, and a fascinatingly gaunt wind-band interlude between Sonatas IV and V, Haydn arranged the piece for string quartet and also corrected and approved a reduction of the orchestral score for solo piano. During his lifetime this was necessary: otherwise no one would be able to hear the music at all except on those rare occasions when the orchestral original or oratorio arrangements could be performed.

It is the string-quartet edition that currently enjoys the greatest exposure and for the same reason as in Haydn's own time: it's inexpensive to produce (and record) and performances are easy to organize logistically. As a quartet, the music is very beautiful and perfectly appropriate for quiet listening, but it obviously lacks the color of the orchestral original, and the final earthquake hardly has the intended impact. The piano arrangement is even less satisfactory. Happily, all four versions of the piece are pretty readily available on recordings, and if you have lots of time and sufficient curiosity, you can choose among them yourself. If only one will do, then get the orchestral version.

Concertos and Notturnos for lire organizzate (1786–90)

Basic Scoring: 2 solo flutes or 1 solo flute and 1 solo oboe,
        plus 2 violins (or 2 clarinets in the notturnos), 2 violas,
        2 horns, cello, and bass (string parts may be multiplied
        at will)

No examples of the *lira organizzata* survive, which is apparently a good thing, since by all accounts this contraption, which combined a bagpipe drone with a sort of hand-cranked, bowed guitar, must have sounded just horrible. It was the favorite instrument of Ferdinand IV, King of Naples, who, when he wasn't torturing his own subjects, fancied himself a "man of the people" and a virtuoso on this particularly weird folk instrument. Never one to waste decent music, Haydn arranged these pieces for solo flute and oboe (or two flutes) when he went to London, replacing the clarinet parts in the notturnos with violins, and it is these versions that are best known today. He also, as previously mentioned, turned the "romance" of Concerto No. 3 in G Major into the famous "military" extravaganza in the eponymous Symphony No. 100. In addition, the slow movement and finale of Concerto No. 5 in F Major wound up in Symphony No. 89.

The extremely limited harmonic range of the *lira organizzata* (all these pieces are in C, F, or G) means that you will not find the same degree of harmonic boldness as in Haydn's other late works, but otherwise the music is fully characteristic of him, with a sunny lyricism that often sounds distinctly Italian (don't forget that Haydn spoke the language, produced many Italian-language operas, and had in singer Luigia Polzelli an Italian mistress). As you can see from the scoring, these are not really orchestral works at all but serenades (the word *notturno* is synonymous) written for an enlarged chamber ensemble. Warm, gracious, and melodically opulent, but also not lacking in sophistication (Notturno No. 5 actually ends with one of Haydn's famous fugal finales), this music makes friends easily and well sustains repeated listening.

London Trios, Hob. IV Nos. 1–4, for Two Flutes and Cello (1794)

These slender but perky pieces have become quite popular since virtuoso flutists such as Jean-Pierre Rampal first got their lips on them and tooted the music into the affections of millions of record purchasers the world over. The exact circumstances for which Haydn wrote these trios are unknown. Ranging from one to three movements apiece, they represent the apotheosis of the kind of genial, dashing, domestic entertainment that took place in music-loving homes all over Europe. This isn't the place to go if you are looking for Haydnesque thrills, but the intimacy and good humor of these trios is irresistible, and they make terrific quiet listening. Music written as a pleasant diversion has nothing to be ashamed of, particularly at this level of craftsmanship.

Three Keyboard Masterworks

Capriccio in G Major "Acht Sauschneider müssen sein" (1765)

Fantasia (Capriccio) in C Major (1789)

Andante with Variations (Sonata) in F Minor (1793)

Haydn's excellence as a composer of solo keyboard works remains one of music's best-kept secrets. It is especially ironic that his achievement is far less well known than that of Mozart, who, despite being the greatest pianist of his age and the undisputed patron saint of the piano concerto, wrote only a small handful of solo works that show him at his best. The reasons are many and varied. As the more famous of the two composers, Haydn's keyboard music was in greater demand by publishers and consumers, offering more opportunities to write for a broad audience. He also enjoyed relationships with some extremely talented amateur players, whose gifts he was happy to cultivate and challenge. Mozart's best keyboard music consists of the concertos and other works he wrote mostly for his own use. Sonatas and short works for students understandably seldom found him unusually inspired.

Beyond that, both Haydn and Mozart were writing at a crossroads in keyboard history, as the piano supplanted the harpsichord and clavichord as the instrument of choice. Despite the fact that this newcomer demanded an entirely reconsidered technique, composers often could not count on the latest and most modern pianos being available. They had to hedge their bets and make their music playable on the harpsichord as well, which often meant uncomfortable compromises and a style that to modern ears sounds unnaturally thin and deficient in terms of both texture and fullness of tone.

This practical uncertainty was less of an inhibiting factor for Haydn. His nervy, eruptive style, with its bold harmonic and rhythmic contrasts, is less dependent on sheer tone color and textural richness than is Mozart's. It translates well enough, where necessary, from one kind of instrument to another, and while writing for the new pianos offered opportunities of which Haydn was very happy to take advantage, the lack of them was not particularly damaging to what he was trying to express. Haydn's keyboard legacy contains, in addition to the most important piano sonatas before Beethoven, more than a few single-movement pieces that are extraordinary by any standard, and they come from all phases of his career.

The first of the three chosen for discussion here is a rollicking work in free-variation form based on a popular tune, the first line of which might be translated as "It takes eight men to castrate a wild boar" (I'm not kidding). Never mind the subject matter: the tune is indeed catchy. Haydn subjects it to a wildly improbable series of modulations as it winds its way in and out of the musical texture, all in a spirit of good cheer. The much later Fantasia in C Major is a variation/rondo: the ritornello theme never returns the same way twice, although it's always quite easy to spot whenever it reappears. The music's vertiginous high speed, French horn imitations, and funny digressions often sound like an updated Scarlatti sonata, and in two remarkable places, Haydn proves he is writing for a piano by stopping the piece dead in its tracks and asking that the player sustain the note until the sound dies away completely. It's a wonderfully zany ride.

At the opposite end of the expressive spectrum stands the Andante with Variations in F Minor, a grandly tragic work some fifteen minutes long in Haydn's patented double-variation form on two themes—one minor, the other major, both related. The basic tune is a funeral march with a chiming accompaniment, like a foreshadowing of the one in Chopin's famous Second Sonata. Haydn's march is, in fact, every bit as harrowing. He finds room for two complete variations of the minor/major thematic complex, followed by a huge finale that leaps ahead several decades both harmonically and pianistically into the world of romanticism, and to Schubert especially. The ending is absolutely crushing in its grim despair and loneliness. Haydn actually called the work "sonata," but musical scholars have refused to accept this designation with respect to a single-movement in variation form, even though this piece is fully as long as many actual three-move-

nent sonatas of the period. Whatever you choose to call it, do
ry to hear this remarkably intense, dark, and brooding work. It
s unforgettable.

Twenty-four Minuets, Hob. IX:16 (1790s)

*Scoring: piccolo, 2 flutes, 2 clarinets, 2 oboes, 2 bassoons,
      2 horns, 2 trumpets, timpani, percussion, 2 violins,
      and bass*

Haydn wrote a great deal of real dance music, as did Mozart and
Beethoven, and most of it is lost. A few of Mozart's late dances
are well known (such as the famous "Musical Sleigh Ride"), but
this is the grandest and most glorious series of ballroom minuets
ever composed, an entire hour's worth of them, scored for a large
and varied band that Haydn uses with typical panache. No one
knows for what occasion he wrote them, but their wide range
of keys (there's even a strikingly dramatic piece in D minor) and
sheer melodic abundance mark them out as late works, probably
dating from after 1795, when Haydn returned to Vienna from
his second London trip. Because this is real dance music, you
won't find the asymmetrical rhythms and lengthy, sonata-style
developments characteristic of the minuets in Haydn's large
instrumental works, but as so often happens when great artists
face serious practical limitations (and as you already saw in the
Seven Last Words), the challenge seems to act as a spur to inspiration in other directions. There isn't a dull second in these colorful, rhythmically snappy dances, and they confirm Haydn in his
historical role as "the minuet king."

There are many other works that I could have included in this
chapter: some attractive early concertos, the marvelously lyrical
and scandalously neglected string trios from the 1760s (all eighteen of them), and many pieces of light music. But most of these

maintain such a tenuous existence in the repertoire, whether live or on disc, that extolling their virtues might easily become an exercise in frustration should you attempt to find them in order to listen to them for yourself. The truth is, as Dvořák pointed out in a very perceptive essay on Schubert, "the problem with the great masters is that they have given us too much." Certainly Haydn admitted this in a famous exchange with King George III that has been preserved for posterity. He would surely be shocked at the amount of his music that has survived over the centuries. What wouldn't surprise him, though, is just how good so much of it is.

From Tragedy to Comedy

Haydn's War on Blandness

Haydn readily and by choice noticed the comic side of anything, and anyone who has spent even as much as an hour with him will certainly have seen that the essence of Austrian good humor permeated him. In his music this joking quality is very obvious, and his allegros and rondos in particular very often seem designed to tease the listener through capricious jumps from the apparently serious to outrageous comedy, and to indulge an almost wild hilarity.

—G. A. Griesinger

This penultimate chapter looks at the two most important weapons that Haydn developed as part of his ongoing artistic battle against the bland, the dull, and the routine. It is very easy in music to be superficially cheerful, as well as gently sad or pathetic. It is much harder, however, to be truly funny or genuinely tragic, especially in so-called abstract instrumental music without words, where meaning often varies subjectively from listener to listener. And yet, as you will see, tragedy and comedy as defined by the sonata style are very closely related from a technical point of view, taking advantage of many of the same musical elements. Each in its own way represents an opportunity to indulge in the kind of expressive extremes that Haydn, given his love of strong contrasts and his avoidance of literal repetition, found irresistible.

As a comedian, Haydn is generally acclaimed as the best in the business. His achievement as a tragedian remains far more controversial, not because he wasn't good at tragedy, but rather because he was so adept at it that many wonder why he gave it up later in his career. The short answer is that he never did, and a much more intriguing question concerns the rationale for making such an assertion in the first place, in the face of all of the audible evidence to the contrary. I propose to address these issues now because they comprise perhaps the biggest single controversy concerning the expressive qualities of Haydn's music.

However, as a basic principle defining the terms of the following discussion, it is important to remember that there is absolutely no justification for the common prejudice that holds that representing suffering in music is inherently more noble and "deep" than conveying humor and joy. I also ask for your indulgence in granting that words such as *tragic, sad, comic,* and *happy* can be used casually and without literal strictness in describing musical moods, because the point I am going to be stressing is not the difference in shades of verbal meaning as defined in the dictionary but rather the intensity of feeling expressed in Haydn's works.

Haydn in Minor Keys

Beginning roughly in 1766 and continuing until about 1774, Haydn wrote an impressive, indeed epoch-making, series of works in minor keys. He was not alone in this program, although he was one of the first and unquestionably the finest. A whole wave of such pieces overtook central European music, and sometime afterwards, this trend acquired the name "Sturm und Drang" (Storm and Stress), in common with the eponymous German literary movement that actually began later and bears no demonstrable relationship to the musical manifestation. The minor mode, by general agreement, traditionally expresses sadness, melancholy, despair, or tragedy. It tends to be rare in the classical period; rarer still in music intended primarily as entertainment (as opposed to a self-consciously heavy-duty cultural event), and so works in minor keys, particularly those that both begin and end in them, have always been regarded as exceptional.

There is no questioning the crucial importance of the Sturm und Drang period for Haydn, but the more significant question is this: Was it really "about" expressing tragedy, or was something else going on, the result of which was a certain emphasis on music in minor keys? Take a moment and look at Haydn's output during this period:

Major Sturm und Drang Works (1766–74)

Symphonies

Nos. **26**, *35, 38,* **39**, *41, 42, 43,* **44, 45**, *46, 47, 48,* **49**, *50, 51,* **52**, *58, 59, 65*
(19 symphonies; works in minor keys in bold)

String Quartets

Opp. 9, 17, and 20 (18 quartets)
Works in minor keys: Op. 9, No. 4; Op. 17, No. 4;
   Op. 20, Nos. 3 and 5

Piano Sonatas

Nos. 29–41 (13 sonatas)
Works in minor keys: Nos. 32 and 33

Vocal Music

Masses Nos. 3—6
Stabat Mater *(largely in minor keys)*
L'infedeltà delusa

There you have it: thirteen works choosing minor keys as "home." By itself it doesn't look like much, but as a percentage, it's huge. Consider, for example, that Mozart's lifetime minor-key instrumental output in the listed genres contains only two symphonies (out of fifty-plus), two piano sonatas (out of eighteen), and two string quartets (out of twenty-three), and Mozart is much more famous for his sad music than Haydn is. Still, it should be very obvious that these disturbing pieces don't tell the whole story. This was also the period in which Haydn perfected the classical string quartet and wrote his first great (perhaps *the* first great) comic opera. In short, what really happened was that Haydn gradually realized the large-scale expressive potential of the sonata style as it applied to whole works in addition to individual movements, and this in turn gave his music even greater expressive force as well as formal freedom.

If you have the time and curiosity, you can hear this very clearly in comparing the three sets of string quartets, Opp. 9, 17, and 20, all composed within just a few years of each other (between 1770 and 1772). No one knows exactly why Haydn returned to the string quartet in such concentrated fashion after a lapse of more than a decade, but the difference between these serious and sophisticated new pieces and the ten early, breezy quartet/divertimentos of the 1750s is astounding—and the story doesn't end there. Certainly the Opp. 9 and 17 works are fine by themselves, and they were hugely popular in their day. Indeed, Op. 9, No. 4, in D minor is widely regarded as the very first "great" Haydn quartet, but in Op. 20, you will find a still richer variety both of forms and emotional content, so much so that the two other contemporaneous sets were effectively eclipsed.

I am sure you can see that it is not such a large step, conceptually speaking, from having themes and motives interact as part of an ongoing, evolving relationship within movements, to start making these same movements show a similarly dramatic cause-

and-effect response to one another. This does not mean that earlier pieces lacked coherence or effective contrasts. Rather, Haydn discovered how to add an additional layer of what you might call "organizational depth." Finales, for example, are no longer just effectively designed endings in and of themselves; they are the outcome and culmination of an overarching expressive journey (as in Symphony No. 88, discussed in chapter 2). This process inevitably packs a more powerful emotional wallop as well, whether it be happy, sad, or often some combination of the two. The better organized a piece of music is between its movements, the more fun a composer such as Haydn can have within them. Nevertheless the question remains: Why so much music in minor keys? Within the answer lies a unique musical paradox.

Taken in isolation, there's nothing inherently unhappy about the minor mode. The listener's perception of emotion in music is a function of many different qualities—including melody, rhythm, dynamics, and timbre, in addition to harmony—but all of these require one defining foundation to have any impact at all: time. Creating musical feelings of sadness, despair, or tragedy depends not just on being in a minor key but on staying in one. The impact of sorrowful emotions is thus cumulative. You can confirm this for yourself if you recall the finale of Symphony No. 44 (CD 1, track 15), whose fury results from the obsessive repetition of a seven-note rhythmic motive. Over five seconds, it's not so impressive, but over three and a half minutes mostly in minor keys, it's exhaustingly intense.

The same observation holds true for the first movement of the "Farewell" Symphony (CD 1, track 7). Anxiousness and despair acquire immeasurable depth by permitting only the briefest possible contrast with the wistful tune that appears halfway through the development section, eliciting an even more violent emotional response in the relentlessly anguished recapitulation. So here's the paradox: when it comes to the minor mode, expressive intensity arises not so much from the sequence of dramatic events passing through multiple keys that typifies sonata form but from staying put tonally and dwelling on the music's "minorness." No other factor has the same importance in determining emotional impact.

This proposition has an interesting corollary: sonata-allegro form (as distinct from its more general principles) is not inherently geared to the continuous, sustained expression of tragic emotion—or indeed any single feeling to the exclusion of all others. This is why so many nominally happy works (including many by Haydn, Mozart, and Beethoven) reserve their most affecting minor-key sections for slow movements, which are often lyrical, simple in shape, and comparatively stable harmonically, and so offer the necessary time for the minor mode to achieve its maximum impact. Don't get me wrong; tragedy certainly is possible, and figuring out how to manage it in terms of the sonata style was one of Haydn's signal achievements during his Sturm und Drang period, but it took some doing.

What, then, does this say about "happy" music in major keys? Depicting a profound sense of joy, as opposed to mere bland good cheer, requires a higher degree of harmonic contrast (often in the form of repeated excursions to minor keys), so that happiness becomes a quality constantly reaffirmed and defined in opposition to the possibility of sadness. Melancholy music takes advantage of this polarity too—it's not an all-or-nothing proposition—but seldom to the same degree if it wants to preserve its darker emotional qualities. Absent this element of something to "push against," major-key music risks sounding frivolous and trivial.

Once again, you can confirm this notion for yourself in such movements as the opening of String Quartet Op. 74, No. 2 (CD 2, track 1), whose high spirits always exist in close proximity to minor-mode threats (most of the development section), not to mention humorously mysterious harmonic diversions that constantly question where the music is going. Or listen to the end of the first movement of the "Miracle" Symphony, No. 96, whose joyous conclusion comes as a positive relief after the shocking plunge into the minor just before the final bars. In sum, the more convincingly happy the music, the greater its harmonic variety, and this, in contrast to sad music, clearly embodies one of the sonata idea's basic modes of operation: creating drama as a sequence of related events that pass through a wide range of keys.

I leave it to the theorists to explain this expressive dichotomy in greater detail, but the significant point to remember is this: sonata form, by its very nature, regards happy music almost as a "default" setting. That's one reason why pieces grounded in minor keys are so comparatively rare (other reasons include the fact that most composers are not generally miserable and most audiences do not listen to music to be depressed). Using the sonata principle to express tragedy, whether in a single movement or over the course of an entire work, means creating a situation in which an unusual degree of harmonic consistency is desirable, necessary, and does not terminally weaken the feeling of departure and return that shapes the form in the first place.

This is a tall order, and it justifies Haydn's practice in his Sturm und Drang–period pieces of using exaggerated, unusual, and even bizarre musical ideas. These offer such extremes of variety with regard to melody, rhythm, or form that they explain the compensating predominance of the minor mode that produces tragedy. They also affirm the need to integrate the various movements ever more closely, applying the sonata principle to the whole work instead of just select individual parts. Whenever the sections of a large work are very strongly differentiated, tonal stability becomes a particularly important unifying tool. Haydn's "La Passione" Symphony No. 49 in F Minor, for example, displays as wide a variety of sorrowful feelings, from pathos to rage, as there are gradations of mood in his major-key compositions. Its striking level of agitation and fixation on minor harmony are not only desirable emotionally but absolutely critical from a structural point of view as an aid to continuity.

Many of Haydn's Sturm und Drang pieces explore other kinds of extremes: of virtuosity (the horn writing in Symphony No. 51), of exuberance (Symphony No. 48, named for Empress Maria Theresia), or of formal ingenuity (Symphony No. 46, where the minuet returns in the middle of the finale in striking anticipation of Beethoven's procedure in his Fifth Symphony). These are all binding techniques as well, aimed at unifying the four-movement cycle ever more closely, extending the sonata idea to the whole work. In his most significant achievement of the entire period— the set of six String Quartets, Op. 20—Haydn defined both the vehicle and the expressive standard for instrumental music's most profound thinking right up through the present day. The most outstanding quality of these pieces is not the fact that two of them are written in minor keys but that the entire opus successfully integrates such a huge diversity of feelings as well as forms. It represents a veritable "how to" guide to expression in the sonata style. The musical range expands in all directions at once.

It is often said that many composers have a "special" minor key, reserved for their most personal modes of expression. In Mozart, for example, it is G minor, the key of Symphony No. 40, the Piano Quartet K. 478, and the String Quintet K. 516. Interestingly, Mozart's G minor flirtation begins with his "Little G Minor" Symphony No. 25, which was inspired by Haydn's Symphony No. 39 in the same key. Beethoven's proprietary example is C minor, the key of the Fifth Symphony and the "Pathétique" Piano Sonata (No. 8), among other famous pieces. Haydn had a very personal, special minor too, although it isn't often mentioned, because, on the one hand, the Sturm und Drang works claim most of the "minor-key spotlight" and, on the other hand, so few people are familiar with Haydn's entire output in all the genres in which he worked that most simply aren't in a position to comment. The key in question is F minor, and it followed him throughout his life:

Works Featuring F Minor (selection)

Piano Trio No. 14 (c. 1760)

Stabat Mater: "Vidit suum" (tenor aria) (1767)

Symphony No. 49 ("La Passione") (1770–71)

String Quartet Op. 20, No. 5 (1772)

The *Seven Last Words*: Sonata IV (1785)

String Quartet Op. 55, No. 2 (1788)

Arianna a Naxos (1789)

Andante with Variations for Piano (1793)

English Canzonettas: "Fidelity" (1794)

English Canzonettas: "The Spirit's Song" (1795)

Scena di Berenice (1795)

With the exception of the two songs, these are all major works, and the list is by no means complete. Haydn also adopted a sort of "secondary special minor," namely F-sharp minor, a key so unusual that he practically owned it until the twentieth century. It appears in three of his very greatest works: the "Farewell" Symphony (No. 45), the String Quartet Op. 50, No. 4, and the Piano Trio No. 40 (26), whose tragic minuet finale you heard on CD 2, track 11. Note that of these fourteen pieces, only four (*Stabat Mater*, Symphonies No. 45 and 49, and String Quartet Op. 20, No. 5) come from the Sturm und Drang period. Haydn's personal minor tonality both preceded and survived it. Indeed, it is even possible to speculate with some certainty about the precise meaning that the key of F minor had for him, at least a

good deal of the time. Consider these extracts from the texts of
the vocal works:

Stabat Mater: "Vidit suum" (aria—translated from the Latin)

She saw her beloved Son dying abandoned,
As He gave up His spirit.

Arianna a Naxos (aria—translated from the Italian)

Miserable, abandoned,
I have no one to console me.
He who I loved so much has fled,
Faithless and cruel.

"Fidelity"

While hollow burst the rushing winds,
And heavy beats the show'r,
This anxious, aching bosom finds
No comfort in its pow'r.
No, no.
For ah, my love, it little knows
What thy hard fate may be,
What bitter storm of fortune blows,
What tempests trouble thee.

"The Spirit's Song"

Hark! Hark, what I tell to thee,
Nor sorrow o'er the tomb:
My spirit wanders free,
And waits till thine shall come.
All pensive and alone,
I see thee sit and weep,
They head upon the stone
Where my cold ashes sleep.

Scena di Berenice (translated from the Italian)

Do not leave, my beautiful idol:
Across those waves to the far shore
I wish to journey with you.
Increase, O God, increase
Until this excess of grief
Comes to aid me
By taking my life.

All these poems deal with the despair and grief arising specifically from loneliness and abandonment. The clincher, if one is necessary, comes in the *Seven Last Words,* where in chapter 10 you can see that Sonata IV represents the tragic climax of the entire work in the form of a musical meditation on the words "My God, My God, why hast Thou forsaken me?" It has also been suggested that the Andante with Variations for Piano was inspired by the death of Haydn's dear friend Maria Anna von Genzinger (addressee of one of the letters quoted in chapter 3). Opportunities to confirm the expressive meaning of abstract instrumental works are rare, but in this case, the evidence suggested by the word setting is certainly compelling.

Beethoven, it would seem, recognized the special character of F minor in Haydn's work and paid tribute to it three times: in his very first piano sonata (Op. 2, No. 1) from a set of three dedicated to Haydn; in the famous "Appassionata" Sonata (No. 23); and lastly, in the compactly Haydnesque String Quartet Op. 95, No. 11 ("Serioso"). Felix Mendelssohn's last and greatest string quartet, the emotionally intense Op. 80, written (it is said) out of despair at the death of his beloved sister Fanny, is also in F minor, and so is Schubert's indescribably sad and beautiful Fantasy D. 940 for Piano (4 hands), dedicated—very intriguingly—to Countess Caroline Esterházy. Lastly, Chopin chose this key for one of his most famous and emotionally affecting large keyboard works, the Fantasy Op. 49.

The Next Step: Making Music Funny

No one has ever denied Haydn his sense of humor. Often lacking, however, is an appreciation of just how remarkable an achievement this represents. A composer seeking to evoke sorrow need only wallow for a certain length of time in his minor keys, and while the result may not take full advantage of the sonata idea and capture Haydn's special brand of nervous tension or Mozart's inimitable pathos over the course of an entire work, he'll get his point across, aided in no small degree by the popular prejudice that sad music is inherently more profound than happy music. Writing comedy, on the other hand, involves balancing a far more sophisticated range of elements, including dynamic, harmonic, and rhythmic contrasts, an acute sense of timing, and even questions of taste.

Haydn's music was always witty: recall the finale of the early Symphony No. 8 (CD 1, track 14), a deliciously tongue-in-cheek illustration of the phrase "tempest in a teapot" if ever there was one. Also consider the weird and wacky minuet of Symphony No. 28, with its main theme built out of *bariolage* (playing the same note on two strings alternately) and its Gypsy-waltz trio section; or check out the joking pianissimo ending of Symphony No. 23. Nevertheless, simultaneously with his creation of tragic drama within the sonata style, Haydn discovered new comic possibilities to exploit—without, however, giving up either his personal F minor mode or numerous other excursions to the dark side of human feeling.

One of the first of Haydn's overtly comic works is the "Farewell" Symphony (No. 45), the very piece that contains perhaps his most tragic opening. Griesinger, in his biography, correctly describes the finale as a joke, and the fact that the music itself is so sweetly nostalgic only adds to the humor of watching the musicians disappear one by one. This doesn't come across on recordings, obviously, unless you follow eccentric but brilliant conductor Hermann Scherchen's lead and ask the players to say "Auf Wiedersehen!" while making sure that the microphones pick up the sound of retreating footsteps.

In Symphony No. 46, however, composed at about the same time, Haydn wrote an even more incongruous last movement, but one in which the comedy is both purely musical and the result of an extreme, even drastic, formal gambit. The whispered main theme is swift but uncertain—full of unexpected pauses and odd, absent-minded sequences. After a good bit of amiable fumbling about in the exposition and development, the previous minuet suddenly returns in the recapitulation, beginning with its *second half,* as if it had been playing all along and its reappearance were the most normal thing in the world. This thoroughly discombobulates the finale, which hesitates, stops dead, and slinks home in a daze, as if embarrassed by what has just happened. To make his intent extra clear, Haydn marks the music to be played "presto e scherzando": very fast and jokingly.

Haydn's emphasis on comedy, rather than just vigorous good cheer, arises because avoiding formulaic blandness in happy works requires an even more violent scheme of contrasts than does the expression of tragedy. There, the minor mode remains relatively fixed even as it conveys a powerful degree of emotional intensity that sustains the listener's interest and involvement. In major keys, on the other hand, a really volatile mixture of elements of the type that Haydn typically offers, no matter how ear-catching they may be, tends to break up the form (witness Symphony No. 46) and so risks making the music sound like a collection of unexplained, gratuitous effects—a potpourri of isolated incidents devoid of unity or purpose.

To counteract this tendency, Haydn adopts a dual strategy. First, as in his tragic pieces, he establishes a coherent tonal trajectory for the whole work and employs a network of shared motives and ideas of the variety discussed in chapter 2 in connection with Symphony No. 88. This binds the movements together at various levels, both conscious and subconscious. Then he starts cracking jokes. A joke or a riddle, after all, ends with a punch line, which in musical terms represents the resolution of a prior buildup of tension and suspense. Haydn's musical jests are, in essence, *explanations,* and they satisfy in two ways: first formally, by justifying whatever activity precedes them (however seemingly incongruous it may be), and second emotionally, by rewarding the listener's attention with a genuine expressive payoff as pungent in its way as tragedy, if at the opposite extreme of feeling.

Haydn's comic style thus avails itself of exactly the same elements that he uses in tragic music, only mixed and balanced somewhat differently, and it guarantees that the listener will feel a work's underlying sense no matter how crazy things get from moment to moment. This means that he did *not* leave the Sturm und Drang behind when he decided to master musical humor. On the contrary, he incorporated large swathes of it into his new-found technique. The scale of the transformation may be unprecedented, but the procedure flows naturally from Haydn's ability to take individual themes and make them express widely differing, even opposing, moods. Here he does it wholesale, revealing a tragic musical syntax to be a joking one as well and confirming the fact that both stem from a single, consistently used vocabulary of themes, motives, rhythms, gestures, and other types of ideas—a language specifically designed to surprise, delight, and plumb the outer limits of emotional extremes.

Consider, for example, Haydn's way with even a simple gestural element, such as his famously apt use of silence. At the opening of Symphony No. 39's first movement, the pauses that sound so disturbing in an emphatically minor-key context become outrageous when they appear in the first-movement development section of Symphony No. 80 (CD 1, track 6), never mind the finale of the "Joke" Quartet (CD 2, track 7). Similarly, the terrifying syncopated rhythms that propel the first movement of the "Farewell" Symphony (CD 1, track 7) become a delicious farce when they trip up the minuet of Symphony No. 77 (CD 1, track 11). Even counterpoint, in the form of the String Quartet Op. 20, No. 5's gloomy concluding fugue (CD 2, track 8), finds itself the object of laughter in the finale of Symphony No. 70 (CD 1, track 16).

Haydn makes this chameleon-like versatility of his idiom brutally clear in the first movement of Symphony No. 80, where he gleefully mocks the tragic language of his Sturm und Drang period with that sleazy, major-key barrel-organ music. He takes this a step further in Symphony No. 83 ("La Poule," [The Hen]). There, the rhythm of the anguished opening is actually transformed into the poultrylike waddling of the second subject. Tragedy becomes comedy. Even more amusingly, in the first movement of Symphony No. 85 ("La Reine" [The Queen, named after Marie Antoinette, who loved the slow movement]), Haydn quotes the opening of the "Farewell" Symphony, only to have it evaporate into a harmless waltz that leads back to a first subject that can only be called "prissy." Comedy becomes tragedy, only to become comedy once again. The effect of this poker-faced double feint is both funny and emotionally ambivalent, and it inhabits an expressive sphere that is as much Haydn's special province as is the key of F minor.

In addition to harmonic and rhythmic contrasts, Haydn's ongoing explorations opened up an entirely new world of humor in sheer sound—that is, in dynamics and timbre. The most famous example is the "surprise" in the eponymous Symphony No. 94 (CD 1, track 8), but there are many, many other instances of a similar nature, some of them even more startling. The ethereal slow movement of Symphony No. 93, which begins with the dulcet tones of a solo string quartet, gets blown away by a huge bassoon fart so obscene (especially when answered by the ensuing loud, orchestral guffaws) that only the late, great conductor George Szell had the guts to really let it rip on his Sony recording with the Cleveland Orchestra.

On a daintier note, the slow movement of Symphony No. 67 concludes with its main theme played *col legno*—using the wooden back of the bow—and this dry, clicking sound is both arresting and unexpectedly delicious to the point that a Carnegie Hall performance that I saw under Leonard Slatkin (one of the few conductors with the courage to program unknown Haydn symphonies) had the audience chuckling out loud. Anyone who can still get a laugh more than two centuries after the fact—especially from today's decorous modern concertgoers—truly had a comedic gift of Shakespearean proportions. A similar pianissimo joke concludes the finale of the String Quartet Op. 33, No. 4, which ends with an enchanting little tune played pizzicato. You have already heard in the slow movement of Op. 33, No. 5 (CD 2, track 3), how a single pizzicato *plink* completely alters the perception of the music's portentous emotionalism. It was in fact these six Op. 33 quartets, composed nearly a decade after Op. 20, that consolidated the musical language of comedy, and they are just as historically and artistically important as the earlier set.

I have already described some of the melodic games that Haydn plays: strategies such as "When is the tune coming back?" (finale of Symphony No. 88, CD 1, track 4) or "How does the tune really go?" (finales of Symphony No. 68, CD 1, track 12, and

Piano Sonata No. 60, CD 2, track 13). These depend on one of the rarest of all musical abilities: that of writing themes that are funny on their face. That barrel-organ tune in the first movement of Symphony No. 80 is one; the bit of simplistic nothingness that begins the finale of Symphony No. 70 is another. The "ending" that is really the beginning of the first subject of Symphony No. 90 is yet another. You may also want to sample both the first and second subjects of the finale of the "Oxford" Symphony (No. 92), as well as the loony last movement of the String Quartet Op. 76, No. 6, among others too numerous to mention. All the ideas in these pieces are completely distinct and achieve their humorous intent differently.

One disparity between comedy and tragedy, then, which explains why humor is so much harder to master, is that sadness in music deepens over time, but a joke that's repeated too often quickly goes stale. Given the fact that Haydn never repeats himself anyway, he was a natural in this field. No one had a larger repertoire of comic ideas. His inexhaustible facility in coming up with new ones remains his least appreciated quality—probably because these melodies and motives are often asymmetrical and nonvocal in character, even downright peculiar (which is why they are funny in the first place), as well as specifically tailored to their intended purpose. Passages such as the opening of the finale of Symphony No. 70 (CD 1, track 16), for example, make no sense at all out of context.

It was this extraordinary degree of expressive precision, both the very sad and the very funny, that gave Haydn the ability to pursue his war on blandness. The formal solutions discussed both here and in the previous chapters have one purpose and one purpose only: to conquer new expressive and emotional territory across the entire spectrum of human feeling. It would be hard to imagine, for instance, a darker and more disturbing minor-key opening than that of Haydn's "Drumroll" Symphony (No. 103),

but it would be equally impossible to conceive of such pitch black-
ness uniformly spread out over half an hour. When, in the first
movement coda, that doom-laden introduction returns, only to
be laughed off the stage by a speeded-up version of itself, the joke
is as necessary to the emotional and formal success of the piece as
straight tragedy was in those angry middle-period symphonies.
The eccentricity, extremism, and electricity of the Sturm und
Drang era sustain and define Haydn's spirit of comic adventure.
They produce that "wild hilarity" mentioned at the head of this
chapter, and it's no less powerful than the wild hysteria of his
most anguished music.

Conclusion
The Road Forward

O God, how much there is yet to be accomplished in this magnificent art, even by a man such as I was.

—Joseph Haydn

I n the preceding pages, I have done my best to cover all the major issues that will help you get your bearings when listening to Haydn, without oversimplifying things to the point where it does the composer or the music a disservice. The very first piece of Haydn's music that I proposed for listening, the first movement of Symphony No. 90, began with an ending. Taking a page from the composer's own bag of tricks, I would like to end this exploration by suggesting the beginning of another. After all, this book is an introduction to Haydn's work, the first step in a journey that will go on as long as you wish it to continue. So I want to conclude with a little practical advice to start you on your way, and suggest some answers to the question:

Where Do I Go from Here?

On the following pages, you will find four appendices containing lists of all the symphonies, string quartets, piano trios, and piano sonatas (and some other important keyboard pieces). These detail the various numbering systems that you are likely to encounter, dates of composition where known, full work names (including keys and opus numbers as necessary), the complete orchestration of all the symphonies, and finally, an alphabet-coded guide to the recurring attributes, both formal and expressive, shared by many of Haydn's compositions. To further help in making what may seem a daunting task less intimidating, I offer the following answers to FAQs (Frequently-Asked Questions):

Q. Is all this music equally wonderful?
A. Of course not—neither in absolute terms nor subjectively, which is what really matters. However, despite inevitable variations in quality, the amazing thing about Haydn's music is that so much of it really is worth hearing. Among composers who produced works in large quantities, no one's "good stuff" percentage stands higher.

Q. What's the deal with all these different numbering systems?
A. I know: it's a real pain. The symphonies are at least numbered consecutively (but not entirely chronologically), and everyone agrees on what these numbers are, but the order is not Haydn's. However, No. 1 really is No. 1, and No. 104 really is the last of them. Symphonies A and B belong to the earliest batch and were once thought to be string quartets. Speaking of which, the string quartets were published with opus numbers, by which they are still known today, and from Op. 9 onward, these are also chronologically correct. Regarding the earliest quartets, which are really lighthearted divertimentos in five movements (with two minuets each), the opus designations are more trouble than they are worth. Some of these pieces turned out not to be by Haydn at all; others in four movements were found to be symphonies that were turned into quartets simply by leaving out the woodwinds and horns. The ten true early quartets are all listed correctly in

the appendix, and any gaps in the opus numbering reflect this initial chaos.

Both the piano trios and piano sonatas suffer from having Hoboken (H. or Hob.) numbers, which are no longer considered accurate or chronological, as well as more sensible numbering systems reflecting the latest scholarship. I provide both, and you may need to refer to them all (as well as the key of individual works) in order to make absolutely sure you are getting the music that you think you are. In Hoboken's system, the Roman numeral signifies genre—there are more than thirty, but you don't need to know them—while the normal Arabic number refers to the actual work (for example, Symphony No. 17 = Hob. I:17). Yes, it's annoying, but it's really not all that complicated.

Q. Is there anything else I should know about Haydn's take on each of the four major genres covered in the appendices?
A. Only a few very general observations:

In the symphonies, Haydn's use of the orchestra is quite distinctive. I already discussed his frequent use of concerto (or *concertante*) elements, but his orchestral sound has a lean, edgy quality very different from, say, Mozart's. Comparison between the two is instructive. Mozart achieves a warm, sensual sonority by pitting sections of the orchestra against each other, mainly strings vs. winds. He freed his bassoons from merely doubling the bass line, giving his wind band a firm foundation and the orchestra a darker sonority, and he disliked flutes (solo concertos aside), probably because their timbre tends not to mix well with the other woodwinds.

Haydn, on the other hand, treated his players like a collection of soloists. Unlike Mozart, he wanted each instrument to stick out, and his mean sonority is brighter. He pushes his instruments to the extremes of their ranges; loves high violins, flutes, and horns; and even gives the timpani important solos, both loud and soft, in the many works that call for them. Haydn's wider dynamic range and linear, contrapuntal way of thinking create a lean, brilliant sound, and his orchestral strokes of genius, numerous as they are, invariably have a structural as well as a purely sonorous function. Mozart initiated the school of orchestration that led to Weber, Mendelssohn, Wagner, Brahms, and Richard Strauss. Haydn's path attracted Beethoven, Schubert (except the Fifth Symphony, which is pure Mozart), Berlioz, Liszt, Rossini, Verdi, Smetana, Dvořák, and Mahler. Part of the difference between the two schools also has to do with Haydn's openness to popular music (from folk songs to Gregorian chant to ethnic dances), as well as his love of instrumental tone painting, especially the pastoral kind with its imitations of nature. All these factors affect the sheer sound of his orchestral writing.

There is a point of controversy mainly concerning performances of the early symphonies: the presence (or not) of an unwritten harpsichord part. No firm historical evidence supports the notion that Haydn ever required a keyboard instrument in performances of his orchestral works. In fact, what is known generally points in the other direction. Even in London, the observation that Haydn conducted "at the piano" can be explained easily if one considers that the concerts contained both concertos and, more significantly, vocal numbers where Haydn would indeed have directed simple (dry) recitative from the keyboard. The humorous piano solo at the end of Symphony No. 98 makes best sense as a joke if the piano does not otherwise participate (or does so very minimally) until that point, and everyone agrees that the music from the Sturm und Drang period forward does not need any additional harmonic support.

In my view, the presence of a harpsichord is damaging in several ways: (1) in order to be audible at all, it restricts the dynamic range of the other players who instinctively adapt to its limitations; (2) depending on how the player improvises the part, it often imposes a false idea of the actual rhythm of Haydn's bass lines, thus altering the character of the music and making it sound more stiff and mechanical than it should; (3) it's often played by a performer who naturally wants to show off and so becomes a tasteless, concerto-like solo rather than a very discreet accompaniment; (4) it homogenizes the color of Haydn's orchestration, damaging especially the earlier works for small forces by imposing on the music a uniform timbre. Anything that dilutes Haydn's scheme of contrasts strikes me as a mistake on its face, but ultimately this is a point of taste that each listener must decide individually.

Haydn's string quartet scoring also has an open, airy quality quite unlike anyone else's. He wrote, on a conservative estimate, approximately fifty undisputed masterpieces in this medium, an achievement unmatched by anyone else in the history of music. The biggest myth about quartet writing is that the parts are all "equal." In reality, they are all "potentially equal," and while a good quartet composer will see that everyone has a chance to lead at some point, the important thing to keep in mind is that there is always a clear principal voice, even in contrapuntal forms such as fugues. Haydn never forgot this basic fact, unlike so many who came later. His consistently spacious textures—never too thick or heavy—and suppleness of rhythm are a constant source of wonder, and it's impossible to put your finger on any one factor and say, "This is how he does it."

One easily audible manifestation of this special quality: many of the quartets end softly and lightly, in quick tempos, a fact that highlights their greater intimacy, dynamic subtlety, and flexibility as compared to orchestral music. The beauty of the quartet medium, then, lies not in having all four players doing something all the time but in the combinations of duos and trios, as well as passages for the complete ensemble, that create constantly varying colors and densities of sound. Finally, don't be afraid of the early works. They are lovely, even if the huge number of more famous (and arguably greater) pieces that succeeded them understandably gets the lion's share of the attention in concert and on recordings. If you have the time, inclination, or opportunity to try the ten quartet/divertimentos (Opp. 1 and 2) or the Op. 9 and 17 sets, you won't be sorry. For the record, Haydn considered that his "real" string quartets began with Op. 9.

I have already discussed the difficulty of creating great keyboard music in Haydn's day (in chapter 10) and his triumphant success at it. Because he ultimately created the "concert sonata," written for what we would now call a grand piano, Haydn's pieces are often regarded as the connecting link between the great keyboard works of J. S. Bach (and sons) and Beethoven. The piano trios are an even more interesting case. In reality they are "accompanied sonatas." The cello part follows the bass line of the piano almost exclusively, and the violin writing varies in difficulty depending on whom Haydn was writing for. The early trios are often more flashy for the violinist because he had professionals in mind, whereas the late works were intended for amateur pianists—often wonderful virtuosos—with violin-playing friends who were much less so. Once this is understood, the trios are consistently fine musically, often belonging to a higher level of achievement in the early works than the contemporary piano sonatas and even some of the string quartets. The combination of piano with cello on the bass line and violin above is sonically wonderful, even though cellists don't often like to admit it.

Q. What is the best way to put together a collection of "essential Haydn"?
A. The only thing that matters is what you like. If you ultimately purchase the compositions sampled on the two accompanying CDs, you will have a very fine, representative selection of Haydn's best work. In collecting all this music, you will necessarily find

discs coupled with pieces not specifically discussed in this book. When this happens, rest assured that the music will invariably be good, and well worth your time.

Q. What are the top ten qualities that make Haydn sound like no one else?
A. Well, if you insist, and in no particular order:

1. Expect the unexpected: Haydn is always surprising.
2. The music starts "developing" from the first bar.
3. Haydn's forms flow organically from his themes, and . . .
4. No one had a larger variety of themes, and therefore of forms.
5. Haydn had a wider emotional range than almost any other composer, from darkest tragedy to laugh-out-loud comedy.
6. At all periods, Haydn is extremely concise. Even though his later instrumental works are generally longer than the earlier ones, the evolution of his style is not primarily a progress from smaller to larger forms, but rather the discovery of how to pack works of modest length ever more densely in terms of expressive variety and contrast.
7. Haydn introduced spiritual qualities into secular, abstract instrumental music.
8. There is no such thing as "bad Haydn." His level of sheer craftsmanship is unsurpassed: Mozart once said, "Even the smallest trifle reveals the hand of a master."
9. Haydn never repeats himself from one work to the next.
10. Haydn's music is exhilarating: it makes you feel good.

Q. Any final thoughts?
A. Yes, one. It is very fashionable today to question the "great works" approach to the experience of culture, whether from an academic perspective or simply as consumers. Record labels toss out complete editions of everything and everyone on the basis of

the fact that "it's all equally wonderful." Alternately, they devote much time and effort to unearthing neglected "masterpieces" by lesser or unknown composers. Some of this stuff is fabulous, and it's great to have the chance to listen and make up one's own mind. As an avid record collector, I'm in hog heaven. The market has been awash in music for decades and likely will stay that way. Shoppers and concertgoers are spoiled for choice.

However, after many decades of listening to countless thousands of CDs, as well as to composers great and not so great, I can tell you with complete sincerity that the judgment of history isn't always wrong. Haydn, Mozart, and Beethoven were indeed demonstrably better than their contemporaries, despite the fact that Hummel, Czerny, Beck, Cherubini, Vanhal, Pleyel, Dittersdorf, and Cimarosa did create the occasional masterpiece as well and wrote reams of very pleasant, enjoyable music. I have spent a good deal of my own professional time and energy, well beyond these pages, defending Haydn's legacy from what I view as a lack of popular understanding of who he was, what he did, and what it means. I make no apology for this. It has been, after all, a tremendous, ongoing musical (and literary) pleasure.

In writing this book, I am suggesting what I hope you will find an eminently reasonable proposition: If history has in fact decided that Haydn was the founding member of the most important musical school that has ever existed, then why not give him the time and attention he deserves and approach his creations with minds open to what they have to say? Haydn's is "deep" music: the more you listen, the more you hear and the better it sounds. I believe its directness and relevance will astound you, and I know that your own curiosity and love of great music will enable you to explore further, at your leisure, one of the grandest and most bountifully diverse artistic legacies that the world has yet known.

Appendix 1
Symphonies

No.	Key	Year	Name	fl	ob	cl	bn	hn	tp	timp	other	Attr.
			Symphonies (with orchestration in addition to strings)									
1	D	1758			2		1	2				AI
2	C	1759–60			2		1	2				AI
3	G	1759–60			2		1	2				IO
4	D	1759–60			2		1	2				AI
5	A	1759–60			2		1	2				BDI
6	D	1761	"Morning"	1	2		1	2				DEHK
7	C	1761	"Afternoon"	2	2		1	2				DEHK
8	G	1761	"Evening"	1	2		1	2				DK
9	C	1762		2	2		1	2				ADK
10	D	1759–60			2		1	2				AI
11	E	1759–60			2		1	2				BI
12	E	1763			2		1	2				AHK
13	D	1763		1	2		1	4		Yes		DHKO
14	A	1761–62			2		1	2				DK
15	D	1759–60			2		1	2				BDEGI
16	B-flat	1759–60			2		1	2				ADIO
17	F	1759–60			2		1	2				AI
18	G	1759–60			2		1	2				ABI
19	D	1759–60			2		1	2				AI
20	C	1759–60			2		1	2	2	Yes		CI

continued

No.	Key	Year	Name	fl	ob	cl	bn	hn	tp	timp	other	Attr.
21	A	1764			2	—	1	2				BK
22	E-flat	1764	"Philosopher"			—	1	2			2 Eh	BDKM
23	G	1764			2	—	1	2				KO
24	D	1764		1	2	—	1	2				DHKM
25	C	1762			2	—	1	2				AEGK
26	D minor	1768–69	"Lamentazione"		2	—	1	2				AHJKM
27	G	1759–60			2	—	1	2				AI
28	A	1765			2	—	1	2				HKM
29	E	1765			2	—	1	2				K
30	C	1765	"Alleluia"	1	2	—	1	2				ADKM
31	D	1765	"Hornsignal"	1	2	—	1	4				DHKLM
32	C	1759–60			2	—	1	2	2	Yes		CGI
33	C	1759–60			2	—	1	2	2	Yes		CI
34	D minor	1765			2	—	1	2				BK
35	B-flat	1767			2	—	1	2				JK
36	E-flat	1761–62			2	—	1	2				DHK
37	C	1759–60			2	—	1	2	2	Yes		GI
38	C	1767–68			2	—	1	2	2	Yes		CJKO
39	G minor	1766–67			2	—	1	4				JK
40	F	1763			2	—	1	2				K
41	C	1770–71		1	2	—	1	2	2	Yes		CDJK

No.	Key	Year	Name	fl	ob	cl	bn	hn	tp	timp	other	Attr.
42	D	1771			2		2	2				JKO
43	E-flat	1770–71	"Mercury"		2		1	2				HJK
44	E minor	1772	"Mourning"		2		1	2				GHJKO
45	F-sharp minor	1772	"Farewell"		2		1	2				DHJKM
46	B	1772			2		1	2				HJK
47	G	1772			2		1	2				HJKLMO
48	C	1768–70	"Maria Theresia"		2		1	2	2	Yes		CHJK
49	F minor	1770–71	"La Passione"		2		1	2				BJK
50	C	1773			2		1	2	2	Yes		CJK
51	B flat	1771–73			2		1	2				DHJK
52	C minor	1770–71			2		1	2				CJK
53	D	1777–79	"L'Imperiale"	1	2		1	2		Yes		EKLMN
54	G	1774		2	2		2	2	2	Yes		DEHK
55	E-flat	1774	"Schoolmaster"		2		1	2				DHKL
56	C	1774			2		1	2	2	Yes		CDHK
57	D	1774			2		1	2				EKLM
58	F	1768			2		1	2				JKM
59	A	1767	"Fire"		2		1	2				JKN
60	C	1774	"Il distratto"		2		1	2	2	Yes		CEFHKM
61	D	1776		1	2		2	2		Yes		HK

continued

No.	Key	Year	Name	fl	ob	cl	bn	hn	tp	timp	other	Attr.
62	D	1779–81		1	2		2	2				KN
63	C	1777–80	"La Roxelane"	1	2		1	2				CKLMN
64	A	1773	"Tempora Mutantur"		2		1	2				HKN
65	A	1772–73			2		1	2				JKMN
66	B-flat	1775–76			2		2	2				HK
67	F	1775–76			2		2	2				DHKMN
68	B-flat	1774–75			2		2	2				GHK
69	C	1775–76	"Laudon"		2		2	2	2	Yes		HK
70	D	1779			2		1	2	2	Yes		KLO
71	B-flat	1779–80		1	2		1	2				DEHKL
72	D	1763		1	2		1	4		Yes		DKL
73	D	1780–82	"Hunt"	1	2		2	2	2	Yes		EKMN
74	E-flat	1780–81		1	2		1	2				HK
75	D	1779		1	2		1	2	2	Yes		DEHKL
76	E-flat	1782		1	2		2	2				HKL
77	B-flat	1782		1	2		2	2				KLO
78	C minor	1782		1	2		2	2				HK
79	F	1784		1	2		2	2				HKM
80	D minor	1784		1	2		2	2				FHKM
81	G	1784		1	2		2	2				KL

No.	Key	Year	Name	fl	ob	cl	bn	hn	tp	timp	other	Attr.
			Paris Symphonies (82–87)									
82	C	1786	"Bear"	1	2		2	2	2	Yes		CLM
83	G minor	1785	"Hen"	1	2		2	2				F
84	E-flat	1786		1	2		2	2				EFL
85	B-flat	1785	"Queen"	1	2		2	2				DEFLM
86	D	1786		1	2		2	2	2	Yes		EH
87	A	1785		1	2		2	2				DFH
			Further Commissions									
88	G	1787		1	2		2	2	2	Yes		DEFHLMO
89	F	1787		1	2		2	2				D
90	C	1788		1	2		2	2	2	Yes		CDEL
91	E-flat	1788		1	2		2	2				DEL
92	G	1789	"Oxford"	1	2		2	2	2	Yes		DEFH
			London Symphonies (93–105)									
93	D	1791		2	2		2	2	2	Yes		DEHLM
94	G	1792	"Surprise"	2	2		2	2	2	Yes		ELM
95	C minor	1791		1	2		2	2	2	Yes		DFLO
96	D	1791	"Miracle"	2	2		2	2	2	Yes		DE
97	C	1792		2	2		2	2	2	Yes		EHLM
98	B-flat	1792		1	2		2	2	2	Yes	piano	DEHM
99	E-flat	1793		2	2	2	2	2	2	Yes		EH

continued

No.	Key	Year	Name	fl	ob	cl	bn	hn	tp	timp	other	Attr.
100	G	1794	"Military"	2	2	2	2	2	2	Yes	perc.	DEL
101	D	1794	"Clock"	2	2	2	2	2	2	Yes		DEFO
102	B-flat	1794		2	2	2	2	2	2	Yes		DEHO
103	E-flat	1795	"Drumroll"	2	2	2	2	2	2	Yes		DELM
104	D	1795	"London"	2	2	2	2	2	2	Yes		EM
105	B-flat	1792	"Concertante"	1	2	2	2	2	2	Yes		DF
			Two Early Un-numbered Symphonies									
A	B-flat	1759–60			2		1	2				AI
B	B-flat	1759–60			2		1	2				GI

Attributes

A = symphonies in three movements
B = symphonies in church sonata form (opening slow movement)
C = symphonies with horns in C-alto (high)
D = symphonies with prominent concertante parts for various soloists
E = symphonies with slow first-movement introductions
F = symphonies ending with three repeated chords
G = symphonies with the minuet second
H = symphonies with adagios
I = the Morzin (earliest) symphonies
J = the Sturm und Drang symphonies
K = the Esterházy symphonies
L = symphonies with variation movements
M = symphonies using ethnic/folk music
N = symphonies likely derived from operatic/stage music
O = symphonies featuring counterpoint/polyphony

Orchestration Key

fl = flute
ob = oboe
cl = clarinet
bn = bassoon
hn = horn
tp = trumpet
timp = timpani
Eh = English horn
perc. = cymbals, triangle, bass drum
piano = piano or harpsichord
Note: In the early symphonies, some trumpet and timpani parts are optional, possibly inauthentic or may have been added later. I have included them where possible, but actual recordings and live performances may vary. Similarly, most performances will include a bassoon on the bass line whether specifically indicated in the score or not.

Appendix 2
String Quartets

Opus	No.	Key	Chrono No.	Year	Name	Attr.
I	0	E-flat	I	1750s		BC
I	I	B-flat	2	"		BC
I	2	E-flat	3	"		BC
I	3	D	4	"		ABC
I	4	G	5	"		BC
I	6	C	6	"		BC
2	I	A	7	"		BC
2	2	E	8	"		BC
2	4	F	9	"		BC
2	6	B-flat	10	"		ABCF
9	I	C	11	1770		BDH
9	2	E-flat	12	"		BDH
9	3	G	13	"		BDHI
9	4	D minor	14	"		BDH
9	5	B-flat	15	"		ABDFHI
9	6	A	16	"		BDH
17	I	E	17	1771		BDHI
17	2	F	18	"		BDH
17	3	E-flat	19	"		ABDFH
17	4	C minor	20	"		BDH
17	5	G	21	"		BDHI
17	6	D	22	"		BDHI
"Sun" 20	I	E-flat	23	1772		DHI

continued

Opus	No.	Key	Chrono No.	Year	Name	Attr.
"Sun" 20	2	C	24	"		BEH
"Sun" 20	3	G minor	25	"		BDHI
"Sun" 20	4	D	26	"		BFGHI
"Sun" 20	5	F minor	27	"		BDEH
"Sun" 20	6	A	28	"		BEH
"Scherzi" 33	1	B minor	29	1781		DG
"Scherzi" 33	2	E-flat	30	"	"Joke"	BDGI
"Scherzi" 33	3	C	31	"	"Bird"	BDGI
"Scherzi" 33	4	B-flat	32	"		BDI
"Scherzi" 33	5	G	33	"		BF
"Scherzi" 33	6	D	34	"		F
42		D minor	35	1785		ABI
"Prussian" 50	1	B-flat	36	1787		F
"Prussian" 50	2	C	37	"		B
"Prussian" 50	3	E-flat	38	"		FI
"Prussian" 50	4	F-sharp minor	39	"		EF
"Prussian" 50	5	F	40	"		B
"Prussian" 50	6	D	41	"	"Frog"	BI
51			42		"The 7 Last Words"	B
"Tost 1" 54	1	G	43	1788		FI
"Tost 1" 54	2	C	44	"		BFGI
"Tost 1" 54	3	E	45	"		BF
"Tost 2" 55	1	A	46	1788		B
"Tost 2" 55	2	F minor	47	"	"Razor"	AFI
"Tost 2" 55	3	B	48	"		BF
"Tost 3" 64	1	C	49	1790		DFI
"Tost 3" 64	2	B minor	50	"		BFI
"Tost 3" 64	3	B-flat	51	"		B
"Tost 3" 64	4	G	52	"		BDI
"Tost 3" 64	5	D	53	"	"Lark"	B
"Tost 3" 64	6	E-flat	54	"		G
"Apponyi" 71	1	B-flat	55	1793		BI
"Apponyi" 71	2	D	56	"		BF

Opus	No.	Key	Chrono No.	Year	Name	Attr.
"Apponyi" 71	3	E-flat	57	"		F
"Apponyi" 74	1	C	58	"		FG
"Apponyi" 74	2	F	59	"		F
"Apponyi" 74	3	G minor	60	"	"Rider"	B
"Erdödy" 76	1	G	61	1797		B
"Erdödy" 76	2	D minor	62	"	"Fifths"	E
"Erdödy" 76	3	C	63	"	"Emperor"	BFG
"Erdödy" 76	4	B-flat	64	"	"Sunrise"	B
"Erdödy" 76	5	D	65	"		BF
"Erdödy" 76	6	E-flat	66	"		BEF
"Lobkowitz" 77	1	G	67	1799		B
"Lobkowitz" 77	2	F	68	"		DFG
103		D minor	69	1803	(Incomplete)	

Attributes

A = slow movement first

B = works with adagios, largos

C = five movements, two minuets

D = minuet/scherzo second in four-movement scheme

E = movements featuring counterpoint/fugue

F = movements in variation form

G = ethnic/folk music

H = the Sturm und Drang period

I = quartets that end quietly

Appendix 3
Piano Trios

Chrono. No.	Key	Hoboken No. (XV:__)	Year	Attr.
1	F	37	1750s/60s	CF
2	C	C1	1750s/60s	BG
3	G	XIV:6	1750s/60s	CF
4*	F	39*	1750s/60s	
5	G minor	1	1750s/60s	B
6	F	40	1750s/60s	B
7	G	41	1750s/60s	F
8 (Lost)				
9 (Lost)				
10	A	35	1750s/60s	B
11	E	34	1750s/60s	B
12	E-flat	36	1750s/60s	D
13	B-flat	38	1750s/60s	B
14	F minor	f1	1750s/60s	B
15	D	deest	1750s/60s	EG
16	C	XIV:C1	1750s/60s	B
17	F	2	1750s/60s	BG
18	G	5	1784	F
19	F	6	1784/5	CE
20	D	7	1784/6	G
21	B-flat	8	1784/7	CE
22	A	9	1785	EF
23	E-flat	10	1785	E

continued

Chrono. No.	Key	Hoboken No. (XV:__)	Year	Attr.
24	E-flat	11	1788	CE
25	E minor	12	1788	A
26	C minor	13	1789	EG
27	A-flat	14	1790	AF
28	D	16	1790	A
29	G	15	1790	A
30	F	17	1790	CE
31	G	32	1792	E
32	A	18	1793	AD
33	G minor	19	1793	AFG
34	B-flat	20	1794	ADG
35	C	21	1794	ADG
36	E-flat	22	1794	ADF
37	D minor	23	1794	FG
38	D	24	1795	AD
39	G	25	1795	DFG
40	F-sharp minor	26	1795	ACF
41	E-flat minor	31	1797	DEG
42	E-flat	30	1797	A
43	C	27	1797	A
44	E	28	1797	AG
45	E-flat	29	1797	ADG

Attributes

A = trios in fast-slow-fast form

B = trios with minuets in the middle

C = trios with minuet finales

D = trios with ethic/folk music

E = trios in two movements

F = trios with adagios

G = trios with variation movements

* arrangement of piano sonata movements

Appendix 4
Piano Sonatas

Chrono. No.	Key	Hoboken No.	Year	Attr.
1	G	XVI:8	Pre-1766	G
2	C	XVI:7	"	B
3	F	XVI:9	"	B
4	G	XVI:G1	"	B
5	G	XVI:11	"	C
6	C	XVI:10	"	B
7	D	XVI:D1	"	BF
8	A	XVI:5	"	B
9	D	XVI:4	"	CD
10	C	XVI:1	"	CE
11	B-flat	XVI:2	"	CE
12	A	XVI:12	"	B
13	G	XVI:6	"	EG
14	C	XVI:3	"	A
15	E	XVI:13	"	B
16	D	XVI:14	"	B
17	E-flat	deest	"	C
18	E-flat	deest	"	CD
19	E minor	deest	"	CE
20	B-flat	XVI:18	1766	D
21–27 (Lost)				
28	D	XVI:5	Incomplete	
29	E-flat	XVI:45	1766	AH

continued

Chrono. No.	Key	Hoboken No.	Year	Attr.
30	D	XVI:19	1767	AFH
31	A-flat	XVI:46	1767	AEH
32	G minor	XVI:44	1768	DH
33	C minor	XVI:20	1771	AH
34	D	XVI:33	1771	CEFH
35	A-flat	XVI:34	1771	BH
36	C	XVI:21	1773	AEH
37	E	XVI:22	1773	CFH
38	F	XVI:23	1773	AEH
39	D	XVI:24	1773	AEH
40	E-flat	XVI:25	1773	CDH
41	A	XVI:26	1773	BH
42	G	XVI:27	1776	BF
43	E-flat	XVI:28	1776	BF
44	F	XVI:29	1774	CEF
45	A	XVI:30	1776	CDF
46	E	XVI:31	1776	AF
47	B minor	XVI:32	1776	B
48	C	XVI:35	1777	AE
49	C-sharp minor	XVI:36	1777	CF
50	D	XVI:37	1777	AEF
51	E-flat	XVI:38	1777	AE
52	G	XVI:39	1777	AEF
53	E minor	XVI:34	1781	AEF
54	G	XVI:40	1782	DF
55	B-flat	XVI:41	1782	D
56	D	XVI:42	1782	DF
57	F	XVI:47	1788	AE
58	C	XVI:48	1789	DF
59	E-flat	XVI:49	1789	AEF
60	C	XVI:50	1794	AE
61	D	XVI:51	1794	D
62	E-flat	XVI:52	1794	AEF

Chrono. No.	Key	Hoboken No.	Year	Attr.
Miscellaneous Keyboard Works				
Capriccio "Acht Sauschneider"	G	XVII:1	1765	F
20 Variations	G	XVII:2	1771	FH
12 Variations	E-flat	XVII:3	1774	FH
Fantasia (Capriccio)	C	XVII:4	1789	F
6 Variations	C	XVII:5	1790	F
Andante with Variations	F minor	XVII:6	1793	F

Attributes

A = sonatas in fast–slow–fast form

B = sonatas with minuets in the middle

C = sonatas with minuet finales

D = sonatas in two movements

E = sonatas with adagios and largos

F = sonatas with variation movements

G= sonatas in four movements

H = the Sturm und Drang period

CD Track Listing

CD 1: Orchestral Works

1. Symphony No. 88, First Movement (6:40)
   Capella Istroplitana/Barry Wordsworth
   Naxos 8.550287

2. Symphony No. 88, Second Movement (5:34)
   Capella Istroplitana/Barry Wordsworth
   Naxos 8.550287

3. Symphony No. 88, Third Movement (4:13)
   Capella Istroplitana/Barry Wordsworth
   Naxos 8.550287

4. Symphony No. 88, Fourth Movement (3:53)
   Capella Istroplitana/Barry Wordsworth
   Naxos 8.550287

5. Symphony No. 90, First Movement (7:02)
   Nicolaus Esterházy Sinfonia/Béla Drahos
   Naxos 8.550770

6. Symphony No. 80, First Movement (5:37)
   Cologne Chamber Orchestra/Helmut Müller-Brühl
   Naxos 8.554110

7. Symphony No. 45 ("Farewell"), First Movement (5:40)
   Capella Istroplitana/Barry Wordsworth
   Naxos 8.550382

8. Symphony No. 94 ("Surprise"), Second Movement (5:33)
   Capella Istroplitana/Barry Wordsworth
   Naxos 8.550114

9. Symphony No. 100 ("Military"), Second Movement (6:18)
   Capella Istroplitana/Barry Wordsworth
   Naxos 8.550139

10. Symphony No. 86, Second Movement (7:23)
    Capella Istroplitana/Barry Wordsworth
    Naxos 8.550768

11. Symphony No. 77, Third Movement (2:07)
    Northern Chamber Orchestra/Nicholas Ward
    Naxos 8.553363

12. Symphony No. 68, Fourth Movement (5:14)
    Nicolaus Esterházy Sinfonia/Béla Drahos
    Naxos 8.554406

13. Symphony No. 13, Fourth Movement (3:14)
    Cologne Chamber Orchestra/Helmut Müller-Brühl
    Naxos 8.554762

14. Symphony No. 8 ("Le Soir"), Fourth Movement (3:34)
    Northern Chamber Orchestra/Nicholas Ward
    Naxos 8.550722

15. Symphony No. 44 ("Mourning"), Fourth Movement (3:48)
    Capella Istroplitana/Barry Wordsworth
    Naxos 8.550287

16. Symphony No. 70, Fourth Movement (3:08)
    Nicolaus Esterházy Sinfonia/Béla Drahos
    Naxos 8.555708

CD 2: Chamber and Vocal Works

1. String Quartet Op. 74, No. 2, First Movement (5:46)
   Kodály Quartet
   Naxos 8.550396

2. String Quartet Op. 64, No. 5 ("Lark"), First Movement
   (6:34)
   Kodály Quartet
   Naxos 8.550674

3. String Quartet Op. 33, No. 5, Second Movement (4:50)
   Kodály Quartet
   Naxos 8.550788

4. String Quartet Op. 54, No. 2, Fourth Movement (7:07)
   Kodály Quartet
   Naxos 8.550395

5. String Quartet Op. 76, No. 1, Third Movement (2:37)
   Kodály Quartet
   Naxos 8.550314

6. String Quartet Op. 74, No. 1, Fourth Movement (5:37)
   Kodály Quartet
   Naxos 8.550396

7. String Quartet Op. 33, No. 2 ("Joke"), Fourth Movement
   (3:43)
   Kodály Quartet
   Naxos 8.550788

8. String Quartet Op. 20, No. 5, Fourth Movement (3:05)
   Kodály Quartet
   Naxos 8.550702

9. Piano Trio No. 28 in E, Second Movement (2:48)
   Trio 1790
   cpo 999 829-2

10. Piano Trio No. 25 in G, Third Movement (3:29)
    Trio 1790
    cpo 999 828-2

11. Piano Trio No. 26 in F-sharp minor, Third Movement (5:28)
    Trio 1790
    cpo 999 828-2

12. Piano Sonata No. 33 in C minor, Third Movement (3:57)
    Jenö Jandó (piano)
    Naxos 8.553800

13. Piano Sonata No. 60 in C, Third Movement (2:09)
    Jenö Jandó (piano)
    Naxos 8.550657

14. *The Creation*: Representation of Chaos, No. 1* (6:33)
    Capella Augustina/Andreas Spering
    Naxos 8.557380-81

15. *The Creation*: The Heavens Are Telling, No. 13* (3:44)
    Capella Augustina/Andreas Spering
    Naxos 8.557380-82

16. *The Seasons*: Recitative and Hunting Chorus, Nos. 25, 26*
    (5:25)
    Bach-Collegium Stuttgart/Helmuth Rilling
    Hänssler 98.982

17. *Lord Nelson Mass*: Kyrie (4:25)
    Nicolaus Esterházy Sinfonia/Béla Drahos
    Naxos 8.554416

*Sung in German